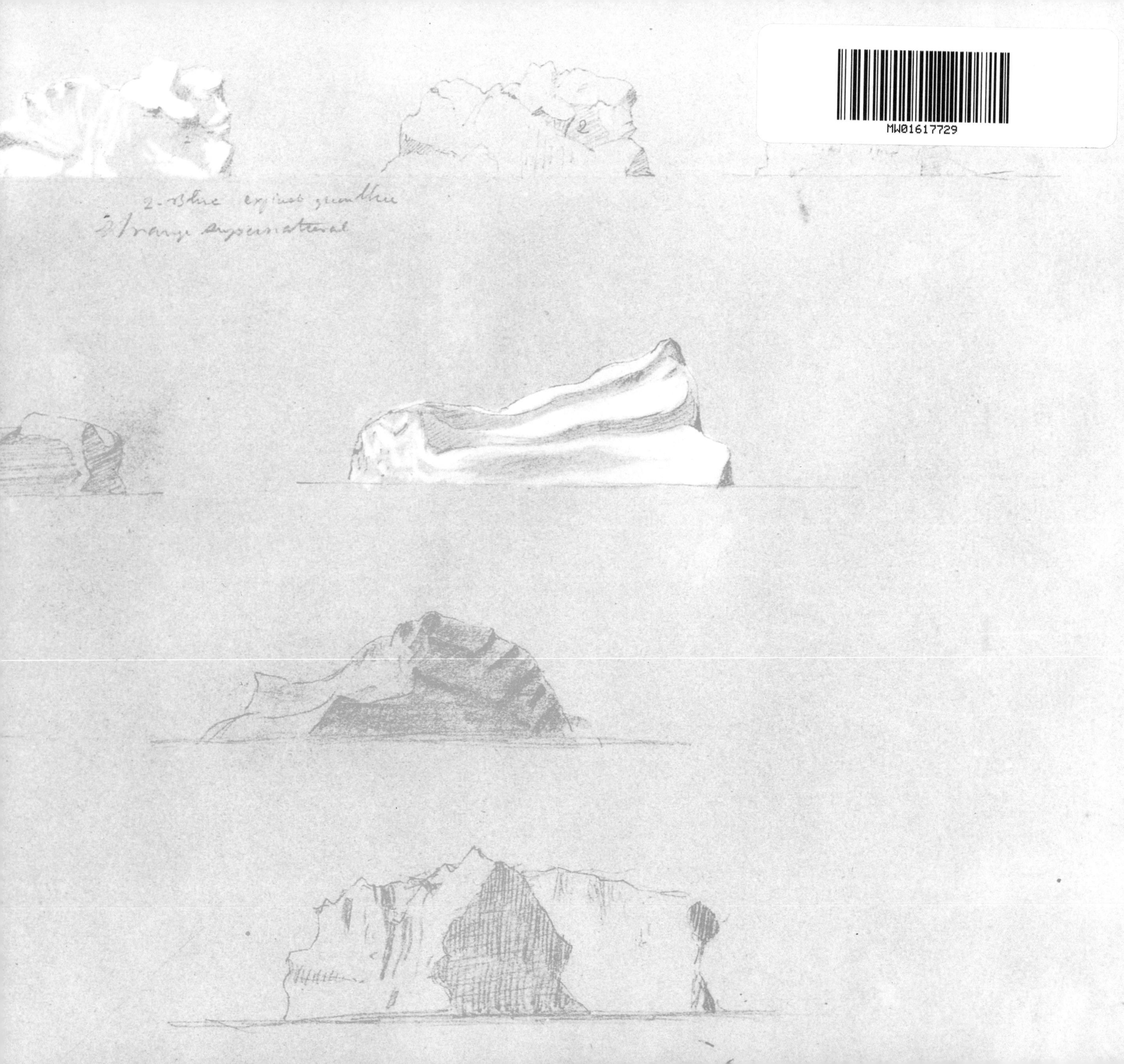
MW01617729

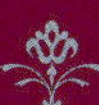

The Icebergs

The Voyage of the *Icebergs*

Frederic Church's Arctic Masterpiece

Eleanor Jones Harvey
with contributions by Gerald L. Carr

Dallas Museum of Art
Yale University Press
New Haven and London

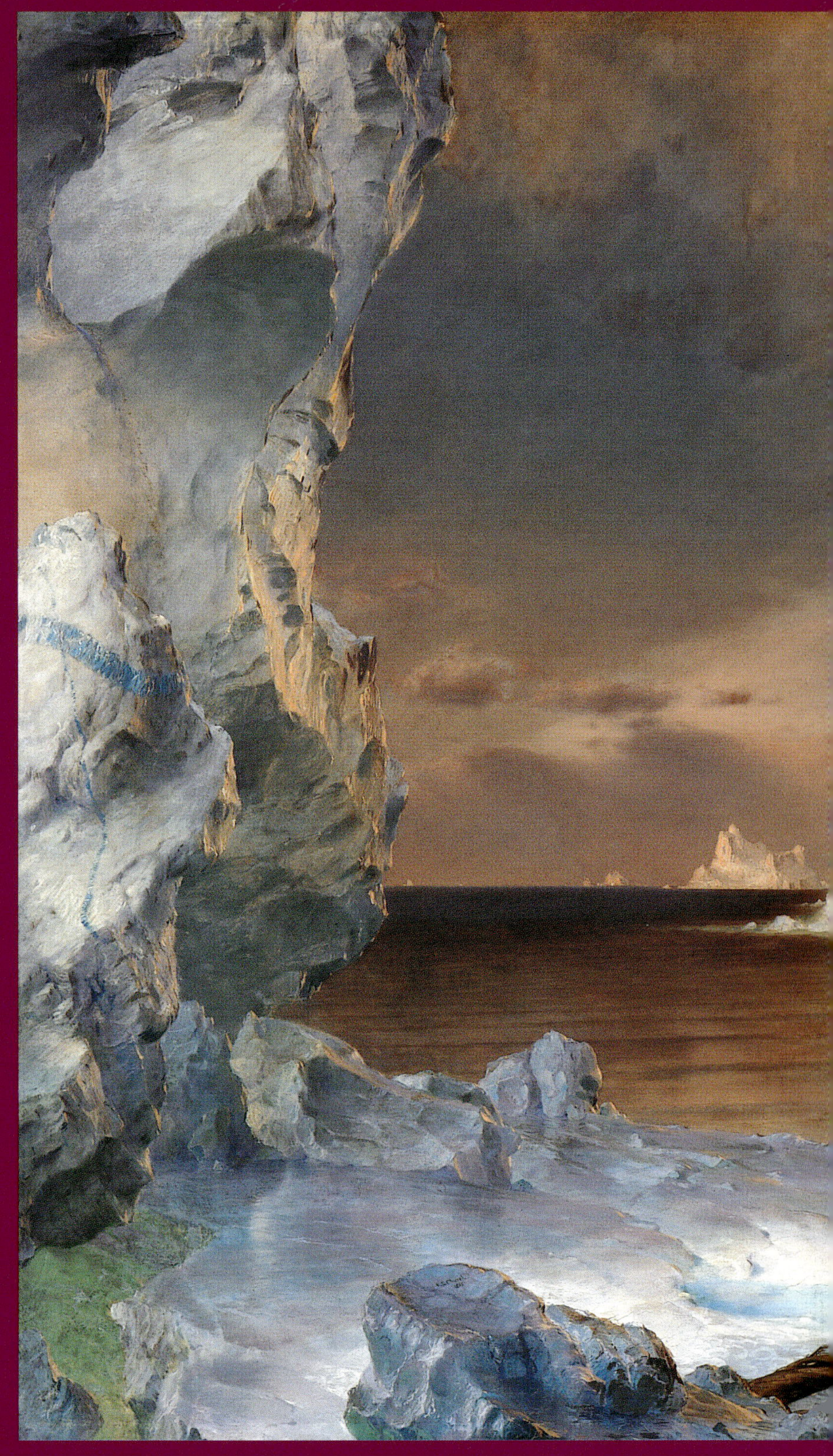

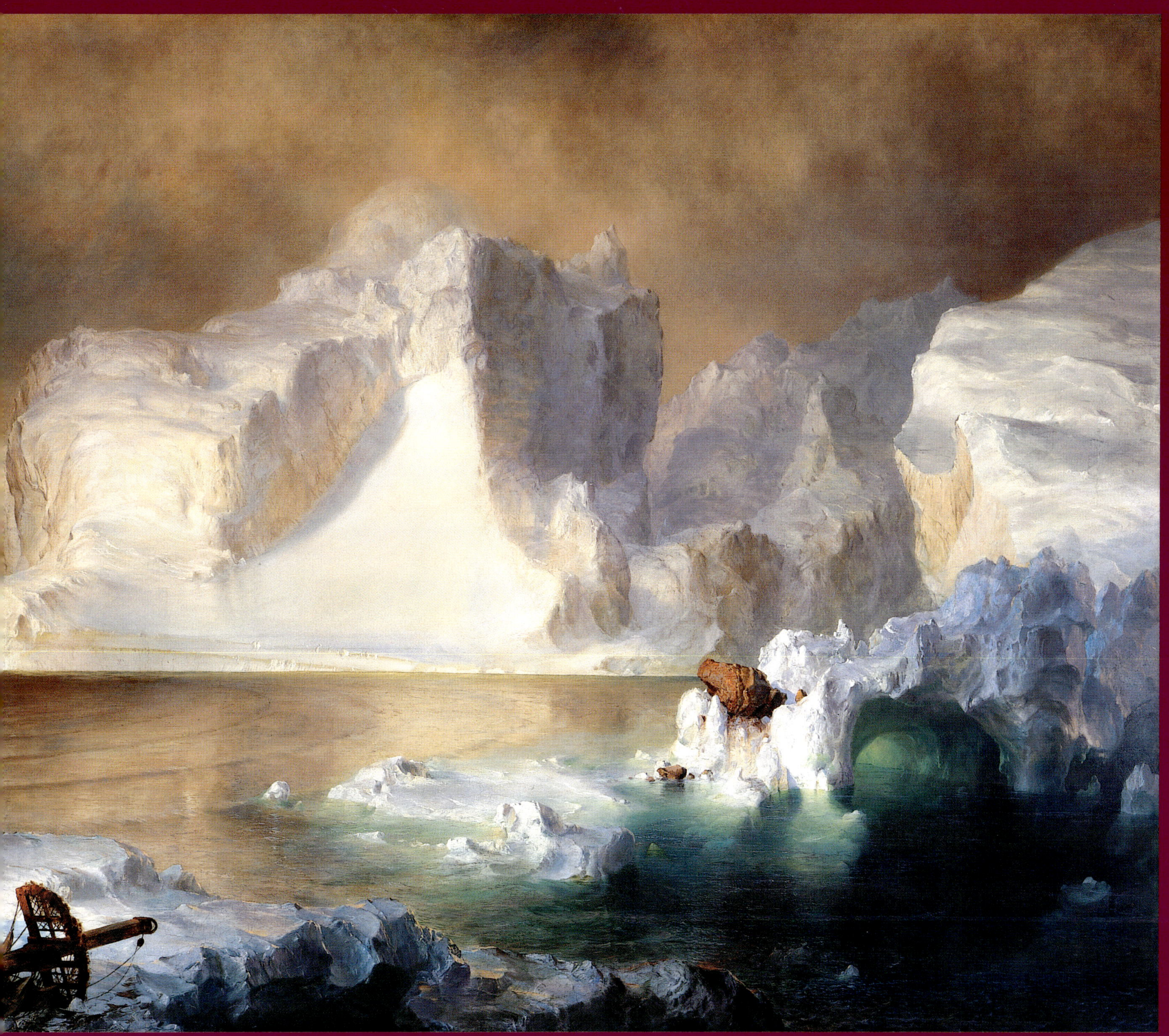

Published by the Dallas Museum of Art. Distributed by Yale University Press.

Library of Congress Control Number: 2002106291

ISBN: 0-300-09536-8

Frontispiece: Frederic Edwin Church, *The Icebergs*, 1861. American, 1826–1900. Oil on canvas, 64½ × 112½ in. Dallas Museum of Art, Anonymous gift, 1979.28.

Endsheets: Frederic Edwin Church, *Icebergs*, July 1, 1859 (fig. 17). Graphite, brush and white gouache on green wove paper, 10¾ × 17⅞ in. Cooper-Hewitt, National Design Museum, Smithsonian Institution/ Art Resource, NY, Gift of Louis P. Church, 1917-4-298. Photo: Scott Hyde.

Curator of American Art: Eleanor Jones Harvey

McDermott Graduate Fellow in American Art: Lyle C. Gray

Head of Exhibitions and Curatorial Publications:
Tamara Wootton-Bonner

Exhibitions and Publications Assistant: Eric Zeidler

Edited by Fronia W. Simpson

Designed by John Hubbard

Typeset by Jennifer Sugden

Color separations by iocolor, Seattle

Produced by Marquand Books, Inc., Seattle
www.marquand.com

Printed and bound by C&C Offset Printing Co., Ltd., Hong Kong

Contents

Director's Foreword

The unexpected but extremely welcome gift of Frederic Edwin Church's *The Icebergs* in 1979 was a defining moment in the history of the Dallas Museum of Art. The sale of the painting at auction electrified the art world, and its subsequent donation to the DMA brought the Museum worldwide attention. Then as now, Church's *Icebergs* is one of the Museum's top treasures. This magnificent painting occupies a singularly enviable niche within the collection: it is popular with the public, highly regarded by art historians in both museums and the academy, and is considered one of the artist's finest works.

It is most appropriate, then, to celebrate this masterwork on the eve of the Museum's centennial, an occasion ripe for reflection on the institution's achievements during its first one hundred years and for consideration of its goals for the next century. The gift of *The Icebergs* was intended to draw attention to the Dallas Museum of Art's permanent collection and to serve as a catalyst for future growth in American art. Since its acquisition in 1979, this magisterial painting has been one of the works of art most requested for traveling exhibitions and has served as a standard by which additions to the collection are judged.

In her ten years as the Dallas Museum of Art's Curator of American Art, Eleanor Jones Harvey has built on this legacy, orchestrating the acquisition of notable works by John Singleton Copley, John Frederick Kensett, William Wetmore Story, Severin Roesen, and Georgia O'Keeffe, adding luster to a collection that continues to grow and improve. Exhibitions and programming play significant roles in building a museum's audience; however, it is the caliber of the permanent collection that, in the long run, determines a museum's importance. This project developed from a J. Paul Getty Trust Grant designed to redirect attention to the Museum's permanent collection through installation and interpretive programming. Dr. Harvey chose to revisit the painting's original debut in 1861 as a "Great Picture," a solo presentation complete with crimson velvet drapes, dramatic lighting, and a printed broadside to enhance the viewer's sense of awe and appreciation of the painting. Her goal was to help the modern viewer understand why our forebears stood in line to pay a quarter (in 1861 currency; today the comparable value would be approximately $5.00) for the privilege of seeing a single painting.

The time was also ripe for an amplification of the painting's history, so ably researched and presented by Dr. Gerald Carr in his landmark book *Frederic Edwin Church: The Icebergs*, published by this Museum in 1980. Dr. Harvey teamed with Dr. Carr to write the current volume, which brings the story of *The Icebergs* up to the present day. In his introduction, Dr. Carr reflects on the impact of Church's painting—on the artist's career, on the market for American art, and on his own career as a scholar. His reconsideration provides a thoughtful capstone to his work thus far on Church and *The Icebergs*. Dr. Carr also compiled the bibliography included in this volume, which is the most comprehensive list of citations to date pertaining to *The Icebergs*. We are grateful both for his words and for his support of this endeavor.

It is our very good fortune to have Dr. Harvey turn her attention to *The Icebergs* on this occasion. Her outstanding scholarship on nineteenth-century American landscape painting, coupled with her particular fondness for Frederic Church's Arctic pictures, laid the groundwork for this volume. Her essays address the creation and marketing of *The Icebergs*, from its inception to its eventual sale in England in 1863, and its "loss" and rediscovery more than one hundred years later. This publication marks the most complete retelling of the painting's return to the spotlight in 1979. Together, these essays consider the power of marketing in both centuries on the fate of *The Icebergs* and on Church's career.

This compelling story could not have been written without the generous assistance of many of the people who were directly involved in bringing the painting back into the limelight, notably Grete Meilman, then co-chair of American paintings at Sotheby's New York, whose memory of the events surrounding the consignment and sale of *The Icebergs* is enduringly impressively detailed; Mair Baulch, then the wife of the administrator of Rose Hill Remand House for Boys in Manchester, England, who filled in many of the gaps in the chronology of events leading up to the sale; and Dr. Sandra Feldman, then a researcher for Hirschl & Adler Galleries, Inc., in New York, whose indefatigable research skills allowed her to locate, if not find, *The Icebergs* months before the rest of the world would know of its existence. To them Dr. Harvey acknowledges her debt and gratitude for their assistance, information, and enthusiasm for the telling of this story.

Many others deserve special mention for their roles, and we are delighted to acknowledge the assistance of the following individuals, in alphabetical order: Ann Berman; Anne Cassidy, New York State Office of Parks, Recreation and Historic Preservation; Dr. Timothy Clifford, Director-General of the National Galleries of Scotland; Stuart Feld, Hirschl & Adler Galleries, Inc., New York; Greg Forster, Rector, St. Wilfred's Church, Northenden, Manchester; Howard Godel, Godel & Co., New York; James Hill and Frederick Hill, Berry-Hill Galleries, Inc., New York; the late David C. Huntington and his widow, Trudy Huntington; Marisa Keller, The Corcoran Gallery of Art, Washington, D.C.; Dr. Franklin Kelly, National Gallery of Art, Washington, D.C.; Roberta Louckx, Sotheby's New York; John Marion; Jay Maroney; Francois de Menil; Ross Merrill, National Gallery of Art, Washington, D.C.; James Miller, Sotheby's London; Harry S. Parker III, Director, Fine Arts Museums of San Francisco; Arthur J. Phelan; Peter Rathbone, Sotheby's New York; Linda Silverman; Dr. Theodore E. Stebbins Jr., Fogg Art Museum, Harvard University; Marilyn Symmes,

Cooper-Hewitt National Design Museum, Smithsonian Institution, New York; Evelyn Trebilcock, Olana State Historic Site, Hudson, New York; Dr. William H. Truettner, Smithsonian American Art Museum; Christopher Weimann; and Dr. John Wilmerding.

At the Dallas Museum of Art, our thanks go in particular to Lyle C. Gray, McDermott Graduate Fellow in American Art, and Mary Leonard, Research Librarian, for their invaluable contributions to this publication. Thanks also go to Bonnie Pitman, Deputy Director, and Charles L. Venable, Director of Collections and Senior Curator of Decorative Arts, for their support for all facets of this project, and to Tamara Wootton-Bonner, Head of Exhibitions and Publications, for keeping the publication on track. Others who deserve particular mention are Giselle Castro-Brightenburg and Michael Mazurek, Visual Resources; Jeanne Lil Chvosta, Rights and Reproductions; and Ana Petrovich, Curatorial Administrative Assistant.

Others who have helped craft this elegant volume are Fronia W. Simpson, copy editor; John Hubbard, Ed Marquand, and Marie Weiler at Marquand Books; Laura Iwasaki, proofreader; and Patricia Fidler at Yale University Press.

Final thanks, as always, go to the anonymous donors of *The Icebergs*, whose unparalleled generosity set a high standard for philanthropy and civic goodwill, providing a painting that numbers among the handful of principal icons in the Museum's permanent collection. The presence of *The Icebergs* at the Dallas Museum of Art is a constant reminder of the abiding power of such a magnanimous gesture. It is to them, with great affection and regard, that we dedicate this volume.

John R. Lane
The Eugene McDermott Director

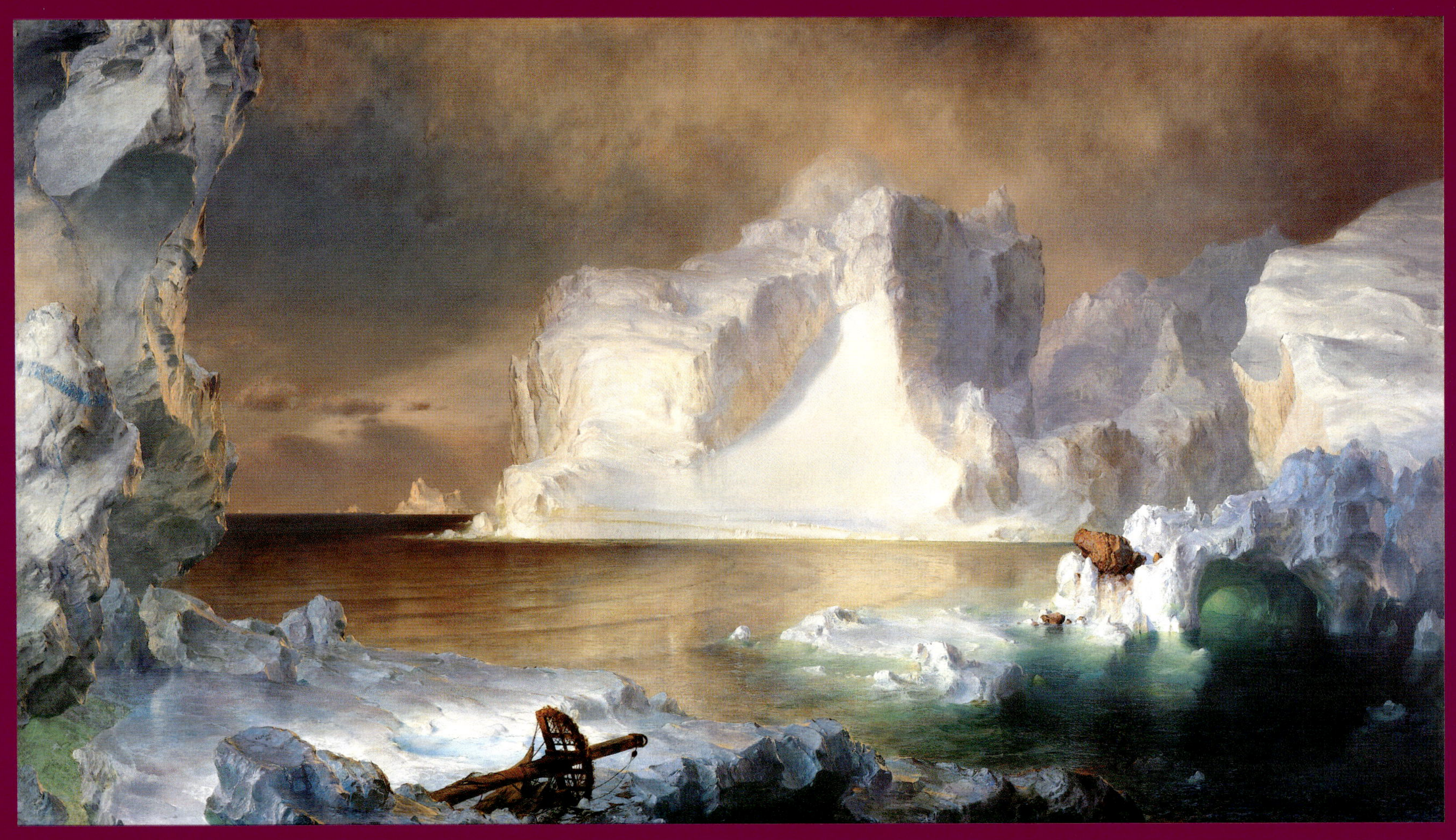

Gerald L. Carr

The Icebergs REVISITED

A Personal Perspective

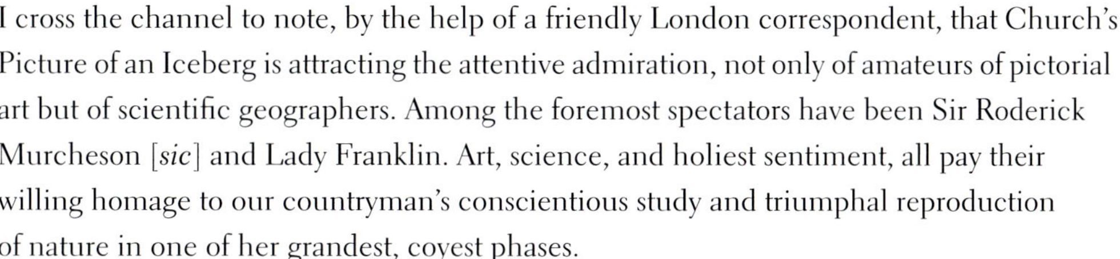

I cross the channel to note, by the help of a friendly London correspondent, that Church's Picture of an Iceberg is attracting the attentive admiration, not only of amateurs of pictorial art but of scientific geographers. Among the foremost spectators have been Sir Roderick Murcheson [*sic*] and Lady Franklin. Art, science, and holiest sentiment, all pay their willing homage to our countryman's conscientious study and triumphal reproduction of nature in one of her grandest, coyest phases.

—"The State of Europe: From France," *New-York Daily Tribune,* July 15, 1863, 3

Frederic Edwin Church's great painting *The Icebergs* (fig. 1), the subject of this book, affirms this epigraph. The story of *The Icebergs* is a kaleidoscope—of talent, adventure, and eye-popping spectacle; of science, colonialism, and multinational wishful thinking; of elitism and popular culture, melded; of shifting Anglo-American alliances; of calamitous times; of subsidence and revival; of sheer serendipity; and, altogether, of riches to rags back to riches. Marking a reinstallation of *The Icebergs* at the Dallas Museum of Art, this publication revisits that tale, initially told in a book I wrote shortly after the Museum acquired the picture, in 1979.[1] In addition, the present volume marks the painting's return to England, for the exhibition *American Sublime* organized by Tate Britain, London.[2] Return, because during most of the twentieth century and one third of the previous one, *The Icebergs* had resided in Britain. The Dallas Museum's Curator of American Art, Eleanor Jones Harvey, and I hope the present book will serve as a libretto or program notes for what was, from its inception, a purposefully theatrical work of visual art. Because images are not necessarily self-explanatory, and because artifacts of all kinds shed their accessibility with age, we hope that our words will open the eyes as well as the minds of present-day and later viewers.

FIG. 1
Frederic Edwin Church, ***The Icebergs***, 1861.
Oil on canvas, 64½ × 112½ in.
Dallas Museum of Art, Anonymous gift, 1979.28.

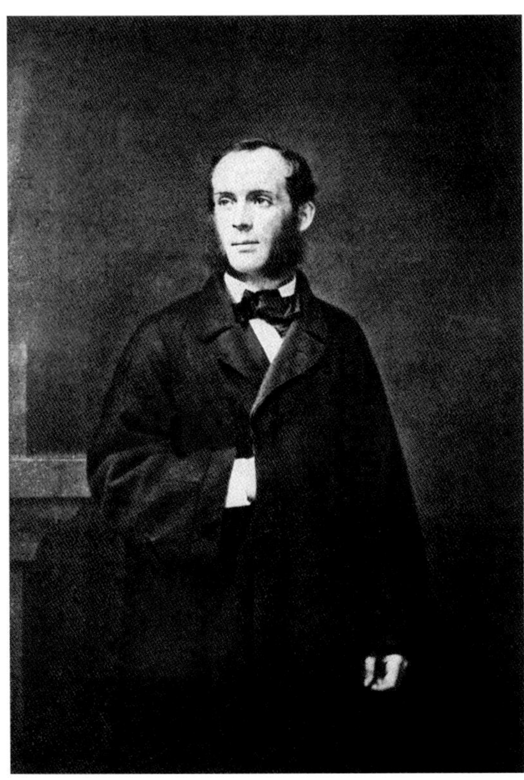

FIG. 2
Mathew Brady, ***Portrait of Frederic Edwin Church***, ca. 1860.
Albumen print, 3 13/16 × 2 3/8 in.
Courtesy, Olana State Historic Site, New York State Office of Parks, Recreation and Historic Preservation, OL.1990.61.

No one was more aware of the blended power of words and images than the man who resurrected Church (1826–1900; fig. 2) for modern audiences. In 1960 the late David C. Huntington completed a pioneering doctoral dissertation on Church for Yale University.[3] A few years later he wrote a landmark monograph, *The Landscapes of Frederic Edwin Church* (1966); co-curated with Richard P. Wunder the first Church retrospective (1966) since the artist's death in 1900; and spearheaded the preservation of Olana, Church's former home in upstate New York (fig. 3), as a public monument.[4]

I benefited from Huntington's knowledge of Church when, from the late 1960s into the 1970s, I was one of his doctoral advisees at the University of Michigan. Armed with myriad color slides (most of which he had taken himself) and with oral ebullience now and then tempered by caveat, Huntington was a proselytizing teacher and lecturer, especially on Church. I recall his counseling listeners that Church's own interests were so far removed from those of modern artists that Church might as well be "an Egyptian." Yet in my book of 1980 on Church's *Icebergs*, I opined that *The Icebergs* was a virile, charismatic work and that it retained much of its original approachability. I would say the same thing today, and more besides. So, which is it? Was Church an "Egyptian" who spoke in tongues and painted in hieroglyphs? Or might he stand so near to us that he materializes alongside and offers voice-over guidance—and hand-holding reassurance—as we confront his images?

As Huntington well knew, the twin fascinations of works of historical art are, first, that they continue to exert influence and to communicate (albeit often in muted tones) long after their creators and zeitgeists have passed; and, second, that changed artistic tastes can change back, and that people accomplish those changes. Church's art had fallen into disfavor even during the final years of his life. Half a century after the painter's death, his creativity and historical ambience spoke to Huntington. I'd like to think that, with his help, that was the case with me, as well.

Excerpted from a period report from the *New-York Daily Tribune* newspaper, the quotation that opens this essay rewinds the clock to a point in medias res. It applauds the two-year-old *Icebergs* and the artist, then thirty-seven. The words nicely capture, and recapture, the moment. Reading them, we can almost hear the (anonymous) correspondent's hands clap as he wrote at his desk. Not yet claimed by a collector, the picture was on display at the German Gallery, a for-hire exhibition space in the West End of London (fig. 4). Shortly before, in 1858 and 1859, respectively, two earlier masterworks by Church, *Niagara*, 1857 (fig. 5), and *The Heart of the Andes*, 1859 (fig. 6), had been shown to acclaim at the same gallery. So far, so good. Leading Victorians interested in the Arctic saw "Art, science, and holiest sentiment" in *The Icebergs*.[5] That's even better. Persons of every social stratum on both sides of the Atlantic who viewed Church's important canvases when they were new—*Niagara*, *The Heart of the Andes*, and *The Icebergs* prominently among them—responded with kindred praises. Portions of that adulation were consciously orchestrated hyperbole. But most were impromptu and, to that degree, authentic. *The Icebergs'* Anglo-American heritage was complemented

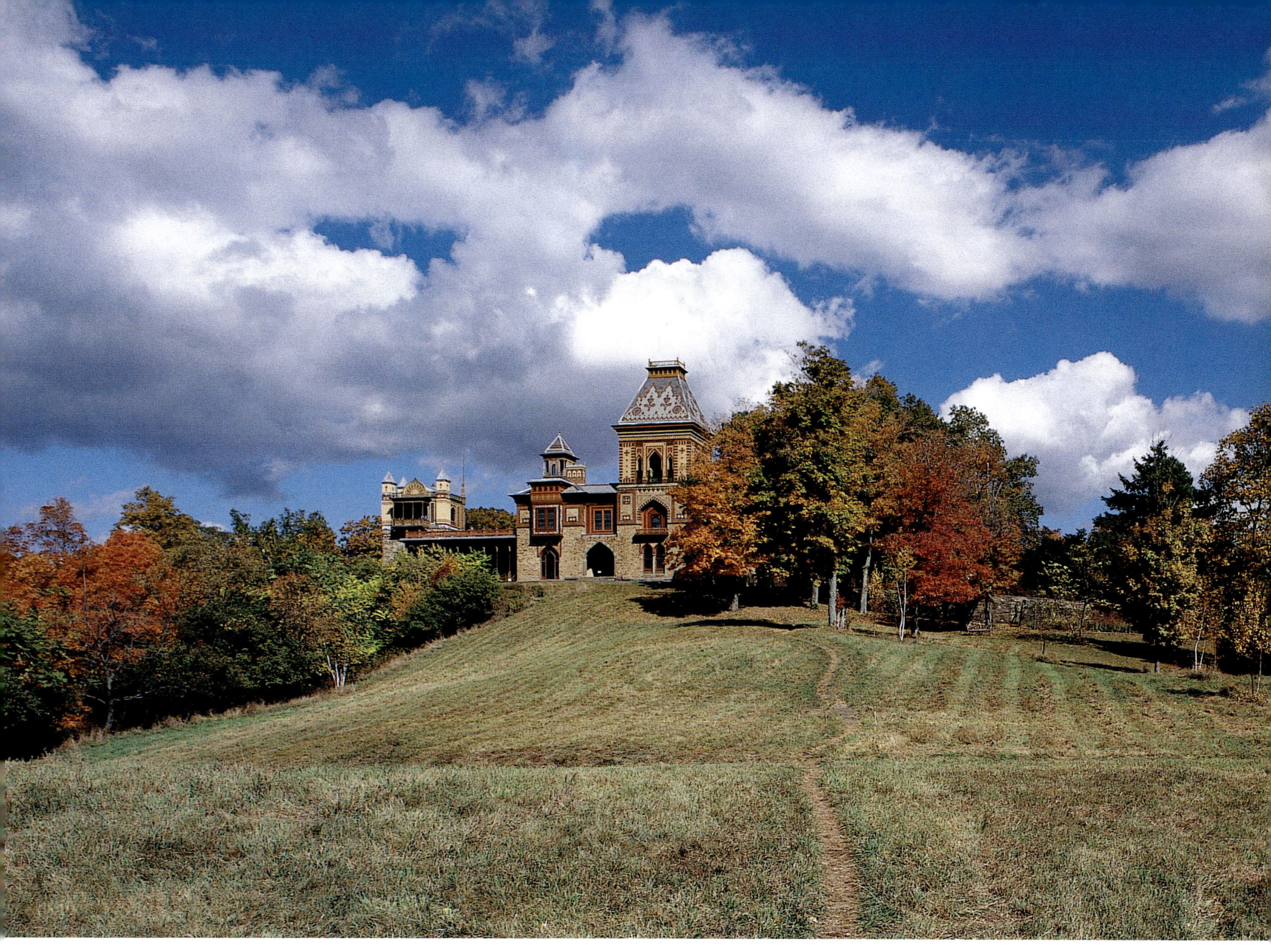

FIG. 3
View of Olana, October 2001.
Photograph courtesy of Gerald L. Carr.

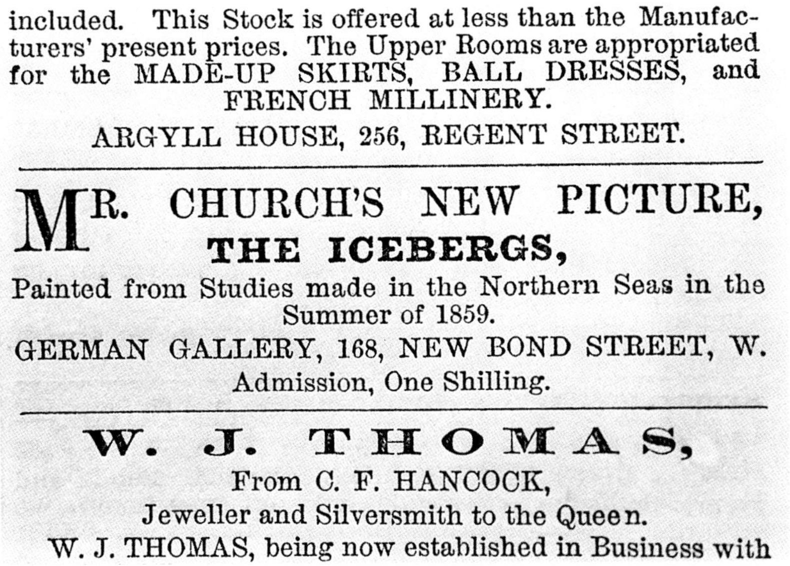

included. This Stock is offered at less than the Manufacturers' present prices. The Upper Rooms are appropriated for the MADE-UP SKIRTS, BALL DRESSES, and FRENCH MILLINERY.

ARGYLL HOUSE, 256, REGENT STREET.

MR. CHURCH'S NEW PICTURE,

THE ICEBERGS,

Painted from Studies made in the Northern Seas in the Summer of 1859.

GERMAN GALLERY, 168, NEW BOND STREET, W.

Admission, One Shilling.

W. J. THOMAS,

From C. F. HANCOCK,

Jeweller and Silversmith to the Queen.

W. J. THOMAS, being now established in Business with

FIG. 4

Advertisement for the London debut of *The Icebergs*, *London Court Journal*, July 4, 1863.

Photograph courtesy of Gerald L. Carr.

by its belated purchase by another prominent Victorian who had an extensive North American constituency of his own. More about that later.

Meanwhile, what shall we make of the *Tribune* writer's workplace, in Paris, France, and of his absorption, at the time, with another topic—the American Civil War? The questions nag because, lifted from context, his summation of *The Icebergs* alludes to Anglo-American affinities and seemingly is stress-free. When the painting was new, however, Stress, with a capital S, encircled and extended far beyond *The Icebergs*—so much so that the efficacy of its imagery and perhaps the canvas's very physical continuance were threatened. The Civil War posed those dangers. *The Icebergs* turned out to be the most topical of Church's big paintings, both in ways he intended and in ways he certainly did not. Were we to peruse it in its entirety, the *Tribune* correspondent's report (datelined Paris, June 26, 1863) would begin to reintroduce the rest of the story.

Church's artistic success, while it lasted, was spectacular. The lineage he embodied was nonpareil. During the mid-1840s he became the first and best pupil of Thomas Cole (1801–1848), the English-born founder of the Hudson River School of American landscape painters. Cole marveled at the teenager's ability to delineate myriad natural forms with pencils and paints. Later, the works of the mature Church were suffused with audacity. He behaved as though no subject was beyond him. In equal measure to Andean volcanoes and jungles, to Niagara, to Arctic "ice-scapes," to the most radiant sunsets in memory and to a passing meteor, and, subsequently, to paradigmatic human sites such as the dead city of Petra, the living city of Jerusalem, and the ruined Parthenon at Athens, Church said, in effect, "I can do that; I can do *all* that." His unquenchable ardor for travel (principally in

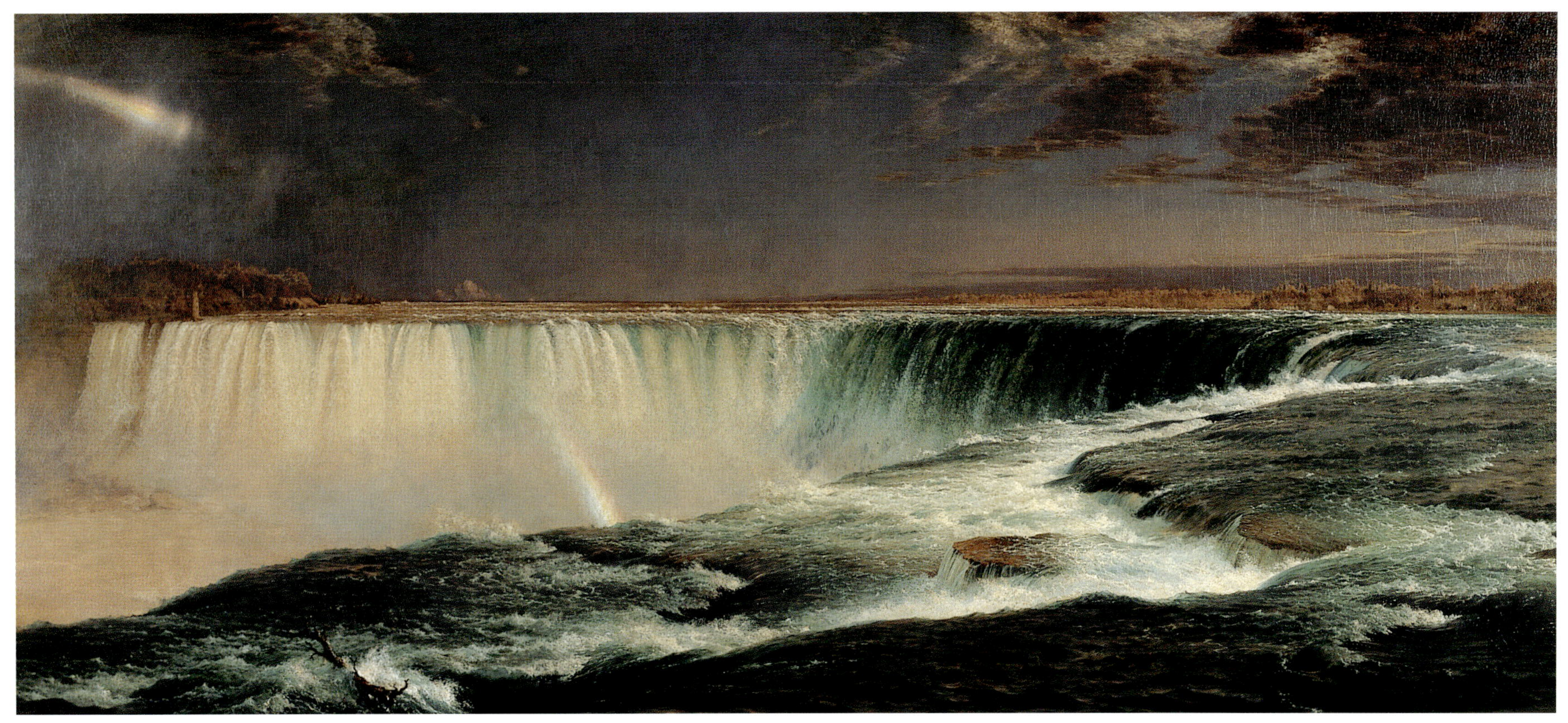

FIG. 5
Frederic Edwin Church, ***Niagara***, 1857.
Oil on canvas, 42½ × 90½ in.
In the Collection of The Corcoran Gallery of Art, Museum Purchase, Gallery Fund, 76.15.

north-south directions) was already legendary within the United States as his career crested during the late 1850s. Starting in 1857, the public releases of his major studio pictures and their touring schedules throughout the East, Midwest, and in Britain became news-making events.

His *Icebergs* responded to the protracted allure of the Arctic. Vast, largely uncharted, but probed by generations of Euro-Americans (some of whom perished or disappeared without trace) and conflictedly claimed by many countries at lower latitudes, the polar regions captivated popular imaginations of Church's day. The fixation can be likened to that of the late twentieth century with space exploration—an analogy, indeed, proffered by a London viewer of *The Icebergs* in 1863.[6] But perhaps most intriguing to us, nowadays, were the propensities of nineteenth-century Euro-Americans to expropriate the Arctic for symbolic purposes.

Americans and Britons did so regularly. For evidence, I cite another noted Victorian, the author and editor (and former newspaper reporter) Charles Dickens (1812–1870)—whose fictional writings Church had read since adolescence—and two additional, anonymous writers for two geographically dispersed metropolitan journals. At a lavish banquet held at New York in his honor during

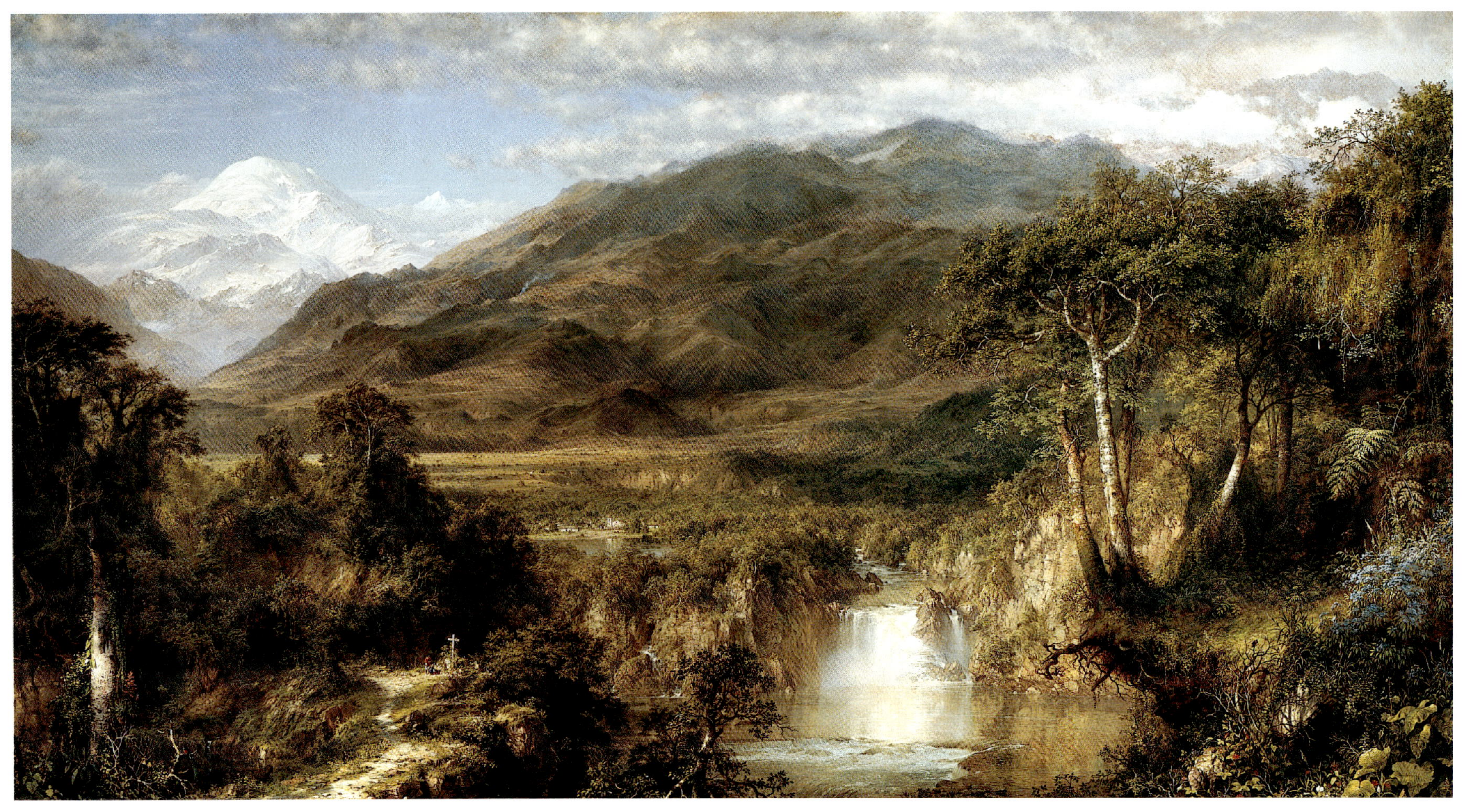

FIG. 6
Frederic Edwin Church, ***The Heart of the Andes***, 1859.
Oil on canvas, 66⅛ × 119¼ in.
The Metropolitan Museum of Art, Bequest of Margaret E. Dows, 1909 (09.95).
Photograph © 1979 The Metropolitan Museum of Art.

April 1868, the visiting English author declared that "it would be better for this globe to be riven by an earthquake, fired by a comet, or overrun by an iceberg, and abandoned to the Arctic fox and bear," than that Britain and the United States ever again collide in conflict.[7] In so saying, he inadvertently epitomized much of Church's artistic expertise to date. Shortly afterward, a London journalist seized Dickens's widely reported metaphor of the earth "overrun by an iceberg." "A splendid conception" it was, he wrote: "Fancy thirty or forty of them [icebergs] rushing about London and Paris drunk and disorderly and throwing whole streets at each other's heads. There has been no such image since the well-known American's description of the boundaries of his country, as being 'On the East the rising sun, on the West the setting ditto, on the North the aurora borealis, and on the South the day of judgment.'"[8] In turn, a London correspondent for the *New York Herald* (a rival

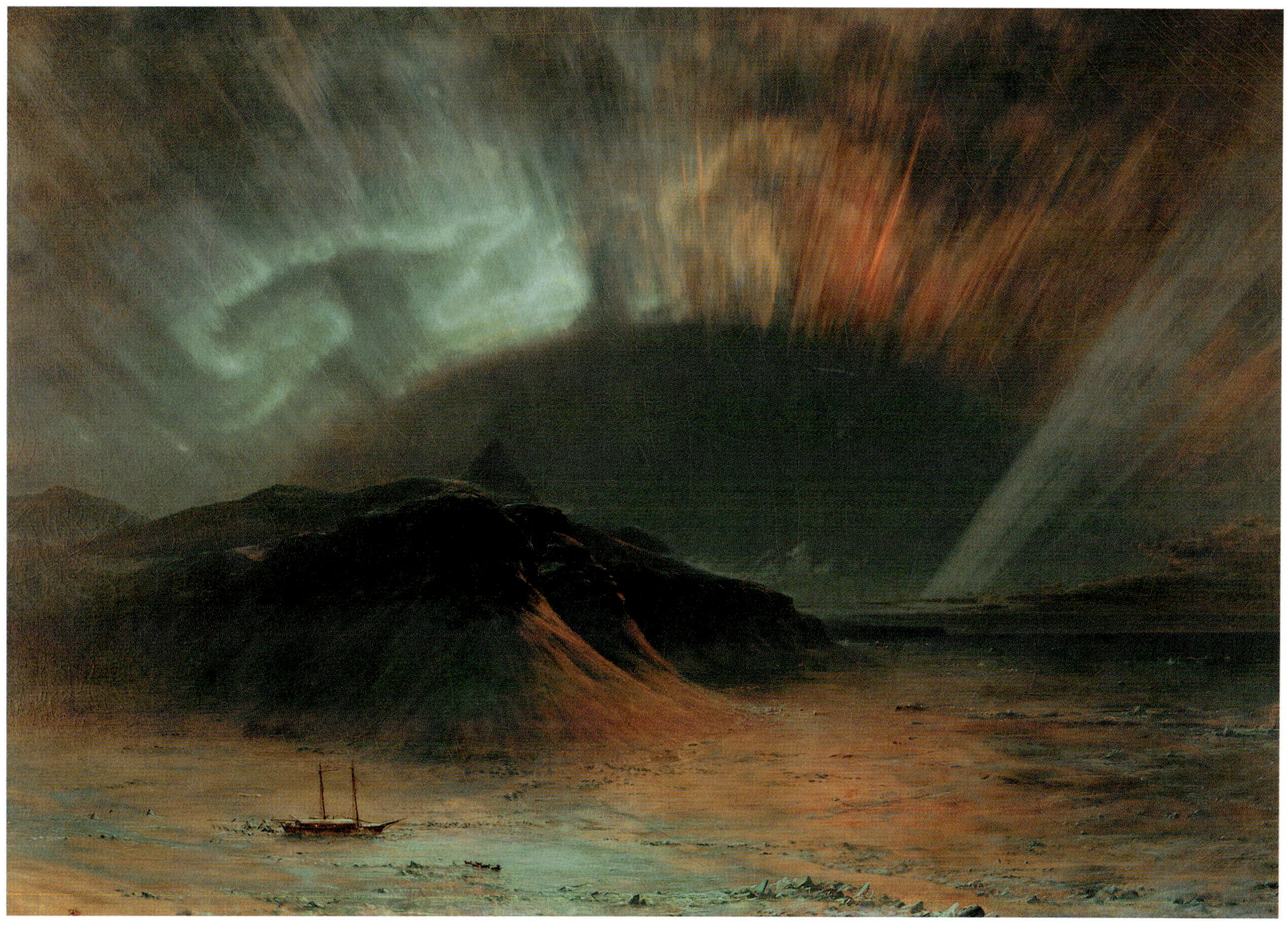

FIG. 7
Frederic Edwin Church, ***Aurora Borealis***, 1865.
Oil on canvas, 56⅛ × 83⅜ in.
Smithsonian American Art Museum, Gift of Eleanor Blodgett.

of the *Tribune*) reiterated his English colleague's Dickensian synopsis for the *Herald*'s readers.[9] Not incidentally, at that juncture (April–May 1868), Church, intent on reformulating his art, was traveling through the Near East into Europe.

These globally encompassing remarks, crisscrossing science and politics, are useful for us because they hint at hypotheses and communication systems implicit in Church's *Icebergs*. The "well-known American's description" of his country's "boundaries" stretching from the aurora borealis —which in 1865 became Church's other Arctic theme for a major studio painting (fig. 7)—to the day of judgment, derived, in fact, from effervescent slogans voiced by expatriate Northern sympathizers in Paris and London during the Civil War, and by throngs of at-home mid-nineteenth-century Americans.[10] And the "splendid conception" of icebergs run amok through northern

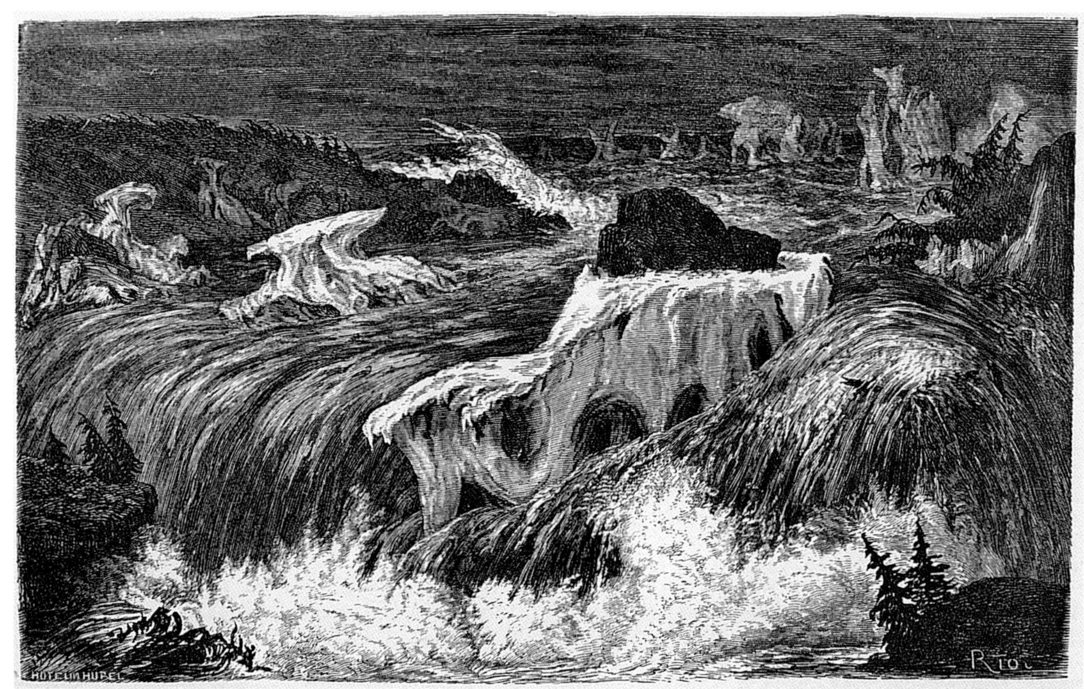

FIG. 8
After Edouard Riou, ***Déluge de nord de l'Europe,*** 1866.
Engraving from Louis Figuier, *La terre avant le Déluge*, Paris, 1866.
Photograph courtesy of the Dallas Museum of Art.

Europe echoed contemporary scientific theories about the earth's early history. The French naturalist Guillaume Louis Figuier (1819–1894) discussed and illustrated exactly that imagining (fig. 8) in his internationally popular book *La terre avant le Déluge* (The world before the Deluge), published in France in 1863 and translated into English in 1865. Church owned a copy of the English edition.[11]

Everywhere that Church's agent, a transplanted Scotsman living in New York, and Church arranged for *The Icebergs* to go—New York City in 1861, Boston in 1862, and London in 1863—during the first two years of its existence, the painting wowed audiences and provoked vivid, varied responses. The *New York Times, Tribune,* and *World* (all 1861) and the *London Times* (1863), among many metropolitan journals, bestowed thoughtful adulation. Out-of-town reports conveyed the excitement felt thousands of miles away. Yet the Civil War affected *The Icebergs* from the outset, starting with its New York unveiling, which took place twelve days after the bombardment of Fort Sumter (fig. 9).

How stifling, and tentacular, was the war for *The Icebergs*? Let's rejoin the *New-York Tribune* report of June–July 1863. Horace Greeley (1811–1872), the *Tribune*'s staunchly Unionist editor (who later introduced Dickens at the feast of April 1868), paired the piece with another American's missive from Turin, capital of the venerable kingdom of Piedmont. Both foreign dispatches clattered with war news—the American one raging between North and South, and others active, or brewing, in

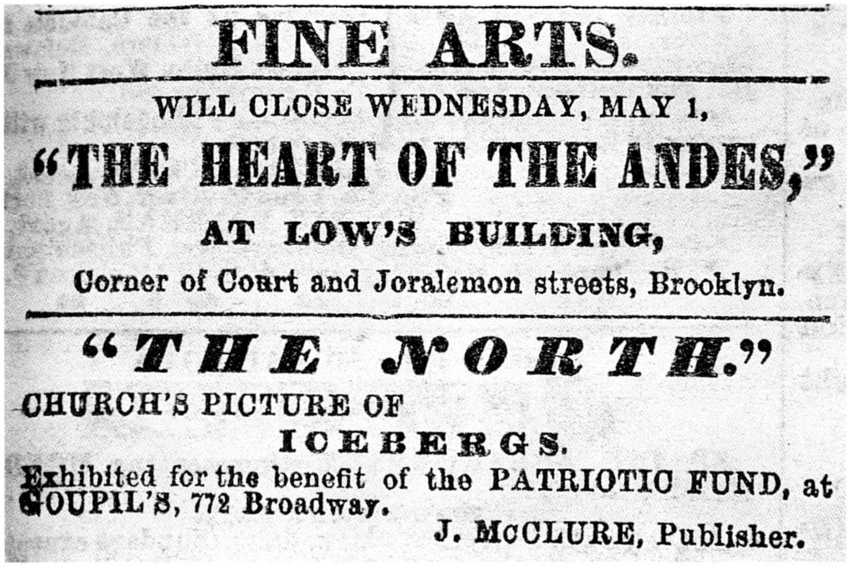

FINE ARTS.

WILL CLOSE WEDNESDAY, MAY 1,

"THE HEART OF THE ANDES,"

AT LOW'S BUILDING,

Corner of Court and Joralemon streets, Brooklyn.

"THE NORTH."

CHURCH'S PICTURE OF

ICEBERGS.

Exhibited for the benefit of the PATRIOTIC FUND, at GOUPIL'S, 772 Broadway.

J. McCLURE, Publisher.

FIG. 9
Advertisement for the 1861 New York City debut of ***The Heart of the Andes*** and ***The Icebergs***, *New York Morning Express*, April 29, 1861.
Photograph courtesy of Gerald L. Carr.

central Europe and Mexico—and war ramifications. The Union cause was not faring well abroad. While emissaries from North and South jockeyed for position in European capitals, governments and journals were capitulating en masse to the "C.S.A."—Confederate States of America. For the *Tribune*'s Paris correspondent, that Southern tilt, although abhorrent, was understandable. Union sympathizers interested in "foreign opinion," he warned, should "sink our ostrich feathers and [instead] raise our heads above the self-sought blinding sands. Nothing has hurt us more than this our constant voluntary shutting of our eyes to our own weaknesses and to the strength of the enemy."[12]

As the reporter also suggested, the concurrent display in London of Church's *Icebergs* briefly pierced the malaise. But in what respects? The writer warmed to hearsay description of what was, after all, a frigid, inhospitable scene, "conscientiously" portrayed. Here, surely, was a resourceful, plucky countryman who was also a realist. Hence, a flagship work of contemporary American—that is to say, Unionist—art, buoyed rather than deflated by "foreign opinion," functioned in two ways. On the one hand, it sidestepped contemporary concerns by instilling among viewers awe, reverence, exhilaration, and gratitude toward its creator, Church. On the other hand, it helped rally Unionist readers of newsprint everywhere. By chance, just as he was concluding his missive, the *Tribune* correspondent was interrupted by "that genialist of men, our brilliantly and justly successful artist countryman, George Boughton, over here on a flying visit from England." George Henry Boughton (1833–1905), a naturalized American born in Norwich, England, who had lately resettled in Britain, subsequently crossed paths with Church in London.

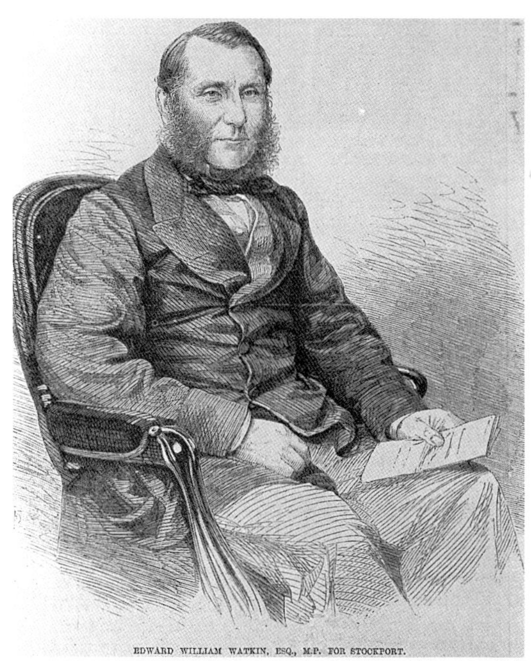

FIG. 10
Portrait of Edward William Watkin,
Engraving from *The Illustrated London News*, July 23, 1864.
Photograph courtesy of Gerald L. Carr.

Thus, in London, while freed from the cumbersome Unionist title (fig. 9) it had borne in New York and Boston, *The Icebergs* retained a measure of intra-American partisanship. Meantime, back home, some American artists from both sides of the Mason-Dixon Line turned hopefully toward Britain for sustenance, much as did French artists displaced by Napoleon's fall, by the French Revolution of 1848, and by the Franco-Prussian War of 1870–71. George Boughton and Church's traveling companion in Ecuador, Louis-Rémy Mignot (1831–1870), for example, moved to London and stayed there. Remaining in America, Church's wartime and postwar quests for British patronage encompassed at least seven of his paintings[13] but bore fruit in a major way only once. As the war was winding down or shortly after it ended, *The Icebergs*, still in England, found a buyer. Knighted in 1868, he was Edward William Watkin (1819–1901; fig. 10), a well-connected, well-traveled English railway mogul, Member of Parliament, and connoisseur. The purchase price he paid is not known, but it must have been considerable, around $10,000. Thereafter the painting settled at the Watkin family country house, Rose Hill, at Northenden, outside Manchester (fig. 11). Church probably met Watkin in London in 1867 or 1869.[14]

But after that, what? A familiar historical irony developed: the transience of fame, compounded by the myopia of nationalism. Something, or someone, that is "up" one day may plunge the next, especially if the object, or person, strays from the place of its, or his or her, origin. Such was the case with *The Icebergs*. For the balance of the century, the unwieldy canvas by an American artist of fading eminence was seen only by those people who visited Mr. and Mrs. Watkin at their Manchester-area home, and by the Watkins themselves. Watkin's first wife died in 1888, leaving him inconsolable and Rose Hill and *The Icebergs* bereft of the social functionalism they had while she lived.[15] After Watkin's own death in 1901, *The Icebergs* more or less sank from sight for three quarters of a century. Luckily, by late 1864, while its éclat was still palpable, the artist's agents had arranged to have the picture reproduced in a sizable chromolithograph in London.

Fast-forward to 1979, a time of revived interest in historic American art. Through a fortunate concatenation of circumstances, *The Icebergs* resurfaced just then. Within weeks of its reemergence in England—at, of all places, Rose Hill, in Northenden—the picture was repatriated (during the 1920s Rose Hill had been taken over by the Manchester City Council and used for various purposes, most recently as a home for troubled boys), whereupon the painting ascended five times in fifteen months to overnight celebrity, all over again. Just as the late 1870s had witnessed Church's final masterpieces of painting, the late 1970s were again propitious for his and his works' revivals. Circumstances were conducive, as well, for people such as me to climb aboard the resuscitation process.

Which returns me to my role in all of this. I should explain that since the mid-1960s I had been a Church enthusiast but hardly an authority. My credentials, however, were good. Starting in 1969 under Dr. Huntington, I had gone to London to work on a doctoral dissertation on early-nineteenth-century London churches—buildings, plural. My escalated involvement with Frederic Church

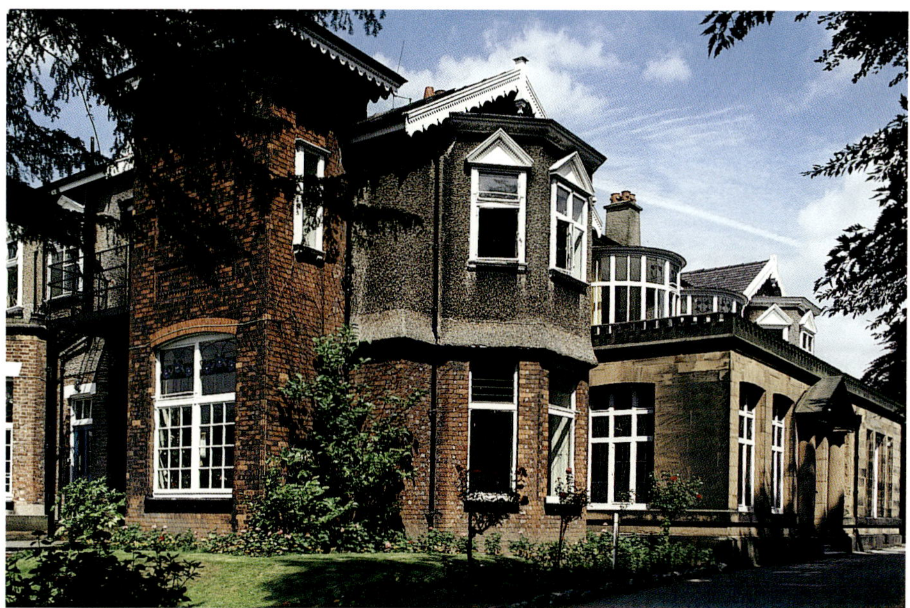

FIG. 11
Rose Hill, Northenden, near Manchester, exterior from the southwest, 1980.
Photograph courtesy of Gerald L. Carr.

began in 1978, during a one-semester leave of absence, again in London, from teaching at Southern Methodist University (SMU) in Dallas. I knew from Huntington's work that several of Church's important pictures had been shown and reproduced in Britain during the 1850s and 1860s, and that the American painter had participated in three world's fairs, two of them held at Paris, into the 1870s. Having delved into late Georgian and early Victorian art criticism for my dissertation, I started scouting Church's European reputation during his lifetime. Within weeks I had unearthed from Victorian journals and books about 140 references to Church and further ones from contemporary Continental and American sources.

Approximately thirty British press reports that I found responded to the acclaimed exhibit (already noted) in London in 1863 of a "lost" painting by Church, *The Icebergs*. While its whereabouts and the initial owner's identity were clouded, there could be little doubt what the "lost" canvas looked like. Three copies of the aforementioned chromolithograph were preserved at Olana. Hoping to foster *The Icebergs'* recovery, Huntington had reproduced one of them in color as the dust-jacket illustration of his *Landscapes of Frederic Edwin Church* (fig. 12) and again among the volume's interior colorplates. At one point during the autumn of 1978, I consulted a Victorian-era reference book that mentioned Sir Edward Watkin's Rose Hill but did not allude to artworks that might be housed there. At another point, I drove to Edinburgh, Scotland, to see a newly reinstalled painting by Church—his largest, measured by surface area—owned by the National Gallery of Scotland since 1887, *Niagara Falls from the American Side*, 1867 (fig. 13). That was my second sight

THE LANDSCAPES OF

Frederic Edwin Church

VISION OF AN AMERICAN ERA

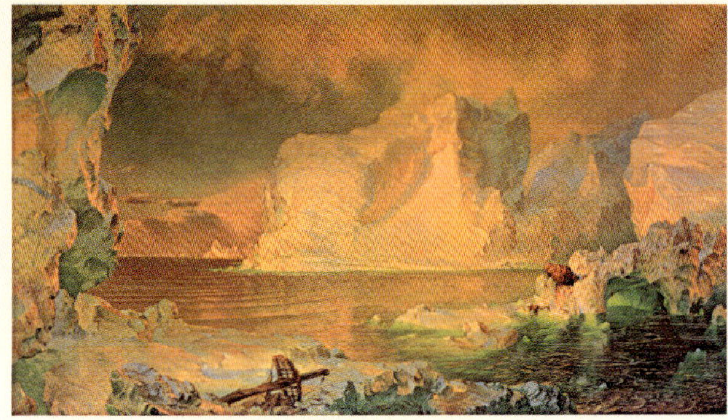

DAVID C. HUNTINGTON

FIG. 13
Frederic Edwin Church, ***Niagara Falls from the American Side***, 1867.
Oil on canvas, 102½ × 91 in.
The National Gallery of Scotland.

FIG. 12
Cover illustration of David C. Huntington, *The Landscapes of Frederic Edwin Church: Vision of an American Era* (New York: George Braziller, 1966).
Photograph courtesy of the Dallas Museum of Art.

of one of the two sizable canvases by Church that had migrated to Britain while he lived.[16] Back in 1971, introduced by my affiliation with Dr. Huntington, I had viewed the 1867 *Niagara*, unframed, in the museum's storage facility. After returning to the United States, I paid my first research visit to Church's former home, Olana.

Ten months later, in August 1979, I happened to be prowling Manhattan when a flurry of reports in American newspapers, among them a second-section article in the *New York Times*, commenced the public phase of *The Icebergs*' rebirth.[17] The painting, the *Times* said, had lately been found in England by Mair Baulch (fig. 42) and her husband, Glen Baulch, supervisors of the home for boys at Rose Hill. In fact, news of the rediscovery and Mrs. Baulch's role in it had been published a month earlier in Manchester and London, but to little notice.[18] The American reports linked the auction house Sotheby's with the picture without specifying its current location. I recall reading the *Times* piece excitedly. Contacting the Sotheby's New York office, I offered my input. Within hours, at Sotheby's local storage facility, I confronted the ten-foot canvas. Superficially cleaned and, at that time, unframed, it made a strong impression.

That October, at Sotheby's fall sale of American art held in its Madison Avenue headquarters, the painting changed the terrain of American art. The pre-auction buzz was amplified by Sotheby's sale catalogue, which contained a foldout color illustration and extended discussion and bibliography of the painting, most of the last provided by Huntington and me. I went to New York to be

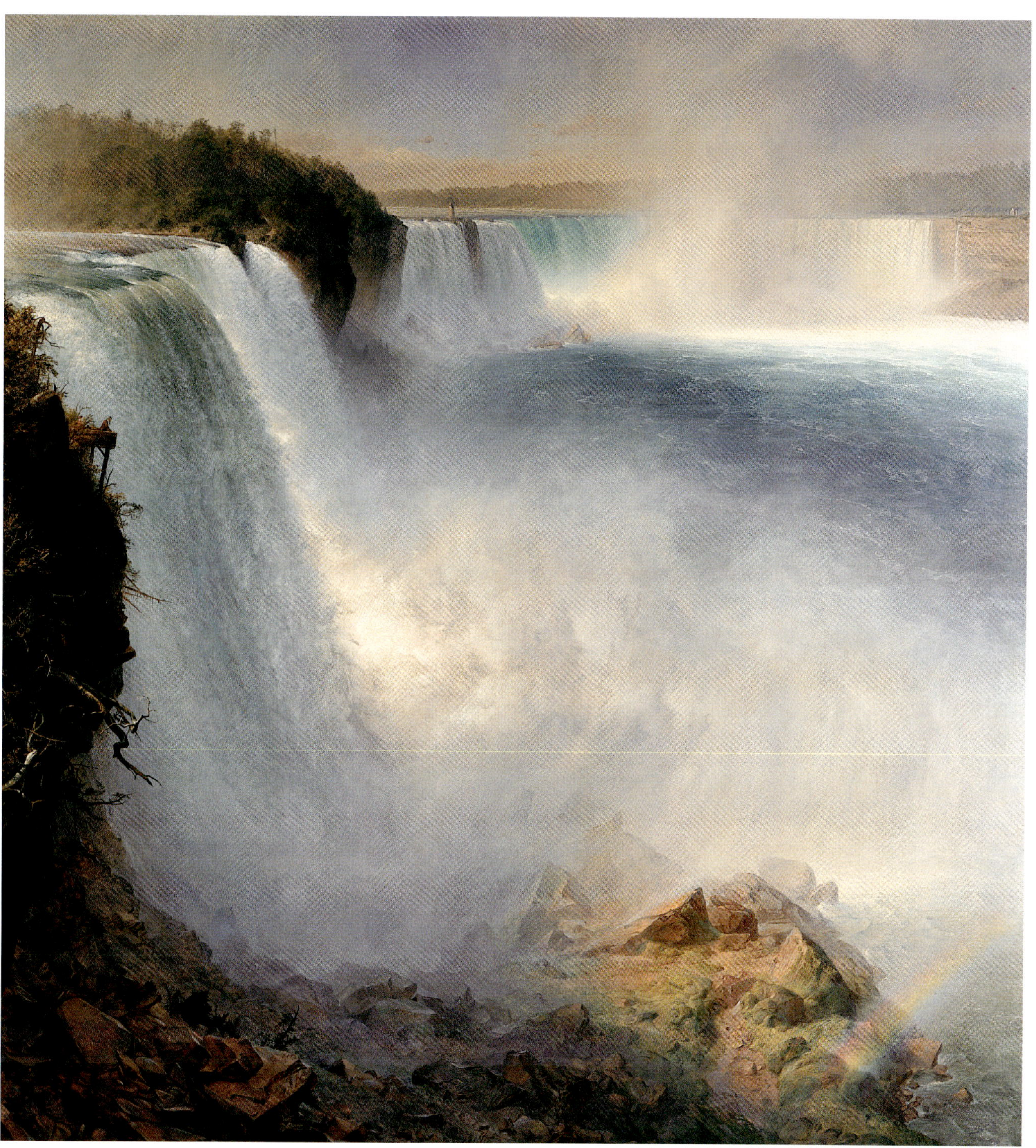

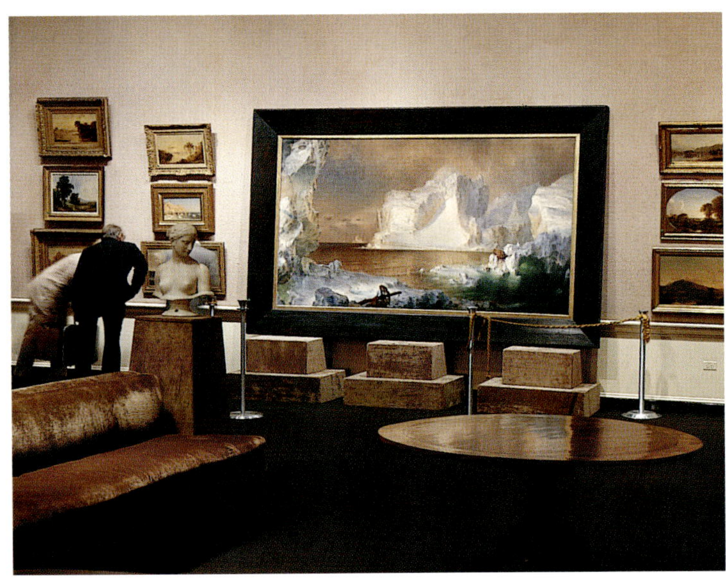

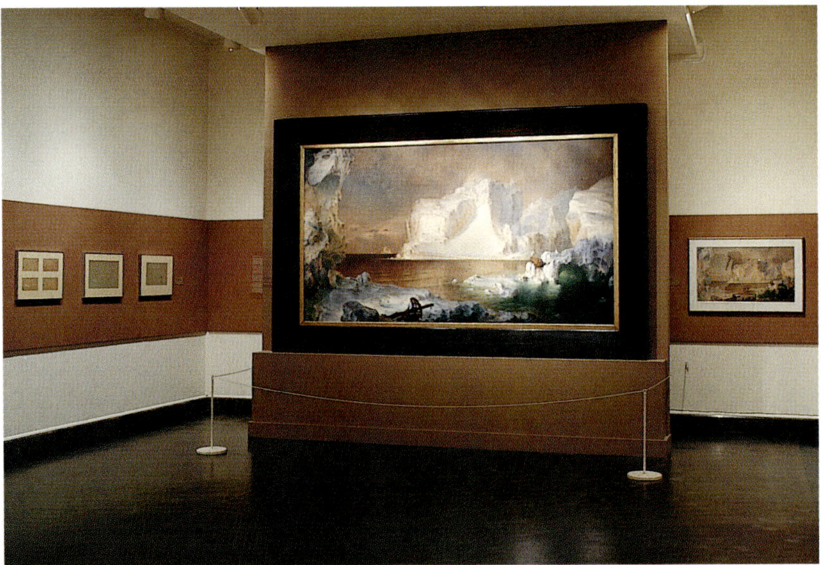

FIG. 14
The Icebergs on view at Sotheby Parke Bernet, October 1979.
Photograph courtesy of Gerald L. Carr.

FIG. 15
The Icebergs on view at the Dallas Museum of Fine Arts, September 1980.
Photograph courtesy of Gerald L. Carr.

present, as did Huntington and numerous aficionados of American art. Two days before the auction, Sotheby's allowed me to photograph *The Icebergs* by available light (fig. 14). At the sale, the audience was stunned as the bidding reached $2.5 million, the third-highest price for a work of art ever attained at auction. Afterward, the mood in the sales room was giddy. As I left Sotheby's accompanied by Drs. Huntington and Theodore E. Stebbins Jr., curator of American art at the Museum of Fine Arts, Boston, and the prime scholar on Church's friend and colleague Martin Johnson Heade, Stebbins turned to Huntington and asked, affably: "Well, what do you think? You created him." Next day, the record-breaking result was headline news in the *New York Times*, across the country, and worldwide.[19]

Initial reports identified the new owners only as anonymous Americans. But within two weeks of the sale, the owners, choosing to remain anonymous, offered *The Icebergs* on long-term loan to the Dallas Museum of Fine Arts (DMFA). Yet more fortuitously, the day the painting went on view there, the owners upgraded the loan to an outright gift. Local press coverage was gratifying. At that juncture, Harry S. Parker III, director of the museum, asked me to write a book about the picture and, separately, to formulate a small exhibition of related works, both for the following year. I, of course, enthusiastically agreed. A few weeks later, *The Icebergs* proved to be the pivotal work in John Wilmerding's encyclopedic presentation of American luminism in 1980 at the National Gallery of Art in Washington, D.C.[20] After conservation in Fort Worth by Perry Huston, the painting was again presented at the DMFA that fall, orbited by satellite images (fig. 15). The book was published a few weeks later.

Since then, *The Icebergs'* renewed celebrity has nurtured American art generally, and the Hudson River School, Frederic Church, and the Dallas Museum of Art in particular. Appropriately, it nudged Church's former home, Olana, as well. Under the capable direction of its site manager during the 1980s and 1990s, the late James A. Ryan, attendance at and outreach from Olana expanded greatly. Among the projects undertaken there was a comprehensive catalogue of paintings and drawings by Church (excepting his architectural studies for the mansion) still at Olana. Authored by me and introduced by an essay by Dr. Huntington (he had died in 1990), the two-volume work is the fullest on Church to date.[21] More recently, on behalf of Berry-Hill Galleries in New York, I organized a touring exhibition of Church's paintings honoring the centennial of his death, escorted by an extensively illustrated catalogue.[22] Both publications discuss polar scenes by Church.

Working at Olana over a period of years, I was privileged to study Church's oeuvre as a whole. Further, much as Huntington had done before me, I responded to the artist's lively romanticism through my own photography.[23] But my two abiding experiences apropos of Frederic Church were of prior date, and both pertained to *The Icebergs.* The later one, a congenial rendezvous during July 1980 with Mair and Glen Baulch at Rose Hill, lasted a few hours. In 2001 I was pleased to become reacquainted with the Baulches. The earlier experience was of a few seconds' duration. In early November 1979 my colleague at SMU, William B. Jordan, told me that *The Icebergs* had, in fact, been acquired by local collectors and that plans were afoot for it to come to the art museum at Fair Park. The painting had followed me home—all the way home, to Dallas.

Notes

1. Gerald L. Carr, introduction by David C. Huntington, *Frederic Edwin Church: The Icebergs* (Dallas: Dallas Museum of Fine Arts and University of Texas Press, 1980).

2. Andrew Wilton and Tim Barringer, *American Sublime: Landscape Painting in the United States, 1820–1880* (London: Tate Publishing, 2002).

3. David C. Huntington, "Frederic Edwin Church, 1826–1900: Painter of the Adamic New World Myth," Ph.D. diss., Yale University, 1960.

4. *Frederic Edwin Church,* introduction by David C. Huntington, preface by Richard P. Wunder (Washington, D.C.: National Collection of Fine Arts, Smithsonian Institution, 1966). The Church show of 1966 inaugurated a surge of exhibitions of Hudson River School painters that continues to the present day. In that respect, Church exchanged places with his master, Thomas Cole, a comparable exhibition of whose works was held at the Memorial Art Gallery of the University of Rochester and other venues in 1969.

The bibliography on Olana is now extensive. See especially Gerald L. Carr, *In Search of the Promised Land: Paintings by Frederic Edwin Church* (New York: Berry-Hill Galleries; Hanover, N.H.: University Press of New England, 2000), 100–106, 119 n. 4; and James A. Ryan et al., *Frederic Church's Olana: Architecture and Landscape as Art* (Hensonville, N.Y.: Black Dome Press, 2001), passim.

5. The two people named in the *Tribune* report are Sir Roderick Murchison (1792–1871), an eminent Scottish geologist, and Lady Jane Franklin (1792–1875), the crusading widow of the Arctic explorer Sir John Franklin (1786–1847). Lady Franklin, who was an aunt of Florence Nightingale, twice visited the United States, in 1860 and 1870, to solicit American support in the search for her husband.

6. Robert Rawlinson, "Icebergs and Meteorology," *London Times,* July 7, 1863, 7. Referring to Church's painting, Rawlinson, an interested reader of the *Times,* hypothesized: "A glance at these floating ice islands may be as instructive as a peep at Jupiter, and a correct knowledge of the terrestrial and atmospheric influences of melting mountains of ice in our Arctic seas may prove them to be as great, if not greater than the terrestrial influences of Mars and Venus in conjunction, or of any single planet or possible combination of moon, comets, and planets at any time." A clipping of Rawlinson's published letter was in Church's scrapbook, formerly at Olana, photocopied by Huntington.

7. Held at Delmonico's and attended by about two hundred publishers, editors, writers, and other dignitaries representing the press across the United States, the banquet took place on the evening of April 18, 1868. The proceedings were extensively reported the next day and thereafter. The fullest account was "Mr. Dickens at Dinner," *World* (New York), April 19, 1868, 1, 8. In addition to the *World* article and that cited below, n. 8, see especially "The Dickens Dinner," *New York Herald,* April 19, 1868, 7; "The Dickens Banquet," *New York Times,* April 19, 1868, 8; "Charles Dickens. The Press Dinner at Delmonico's," *New-York Daily Tribune,* April 20, 1868, 1–2; "The United States. (From an American Correspondent)," *London Times,* May 4, 1868, 5; and the untitled editorial, ibid., May 5, 1868, 9.

8. "Mr. Dickens and the Americans," *Pall Mall Gazette* (London), May 5, 1868, 5. Dickens had had prior, vicarious contact with the Arctic, via a three-act stage play, *The Frozen Deep,* written by his compatriot Wilkie Collins. Accorded a few performances in London during 1857, the production featured backdrops by the eminent British landscape and marine painter Clarkson Stanfield (1793–1867) and a thespian role for Dickens himself.

9. "Charles Dickens' Return—'American Notes' in 1868. The New York Dinner and Bohemianism . . . ," *New York Herald,* May 18, 1868, 4. The report was datelined London, May 6, 1868.

10. The "description" of American boundaries cited by the *Pall Mall Gazette* writer fuses three Civil War–era banquet toasts anecdotally reported by the American historian John Fiske in a lecture he presented in 1879–80, "Manifest Destiny," and published in his book *American Political Ideas Viewed from the Standpoint of Universal History* (New York: Harper, 1885), 101–2. Maxims of similar content were features of Fourth of July celebrations by American expatriates and residents alike and, occasionally, unflattering reporting by English journalists. See especially "Two Days Later from Europe. The English Press on the Fourth of July," *New-York Daily Tribune,* July 17, 1862, 3. I am grateful to Linda L. Stein of the University of Delaware Library for helping to track down the reference in John Fiske's book.

11. See Martin J. S. Rudwick, *Scenes from Deep Time: Early Pictorial Representations of the Prehistoric World* (Chicago and London: University of Chicago Press, 1992), 204–5; Carr, *In Search of the Promised Land,* 80. Church's copy of Figuier's book, like most others that survive from his library, is at Olana.

12. "The State of Europe: From France," *New-York Daily Tribune*, July 15, 1863, 3.

13. Besides *The Icebergs*, the paintings were *Chimborazo*, 1864 (The Huntington Library, Art Collections, and Botanical Gardens, San Marino, Calif.); *Twilight: Mount Desert, Maine*, 1865 (Washington University Gallery of Art, St. Louis); *Sunset in the Tropics*, 1868 (Fruitlands Museums, Harvard, Mass.); *Ruins at Baalbec*, 1868 (private collection); *Salzburg Castle*, ca. 1869 (Sotheby's, New York, May 22, 2002, lot 143); and *The Mountains of Edom*, 1870 (on extended loan from Mr. and Mrs. Allan J. Riley, Snite Museum of Art, University of Notre Dame, South Bend, Ind.).

14. Probably while in London, Church cryptically penciled Watkin's name and London address in a pocket notebook (David C. Huntington Archives, Olana State Historic Site) that he (Church) carried with him to Europe in 1867: *Sir E^d Watkin / Bayswater.*

15. A useful reference to Watkin in later life is the untitled editorial in the *London Evening News and Post*, December 7, 1891, 2; cited in Carr, *In Search of the Promised Land*, 83.

16. The 1867 *Niagara* was donated to the National Gallery of Scotland by its second owner, Scottish-born John S. Kennedy, who had purchased it at auction in New York earlier in 1887. Hence Church was not involved with the picture's migration to the United Kingdom. He was, however, aware of the circumstance and of the attention the painting attracted when installed at the museum. Two clippings in Church's scrapbook (see n. 6) discussed the canvas's acquisition by Kennedy and its arrival and display in Edinburgh in 1887.

17. Laurie Johnston, "2 Britons Find U.S. Artist's Long-Lost 'Icebergs,'" *New York Times*, August 17, 1979, B1. While most American press articles of the same date, including that in the *New York Times*, did not illustrate the painting, at least one ("'Icebergs' Stuns Art World, May Set Record Price," *Detroit News*, August 17, 1979, A12) did so. A few months later, that report facilitated the rediscovery, in a Michigan collection, of a preparatory oil study by Church (twice sold since then and now privately owned) for *The Icebergs*.

18. "The 1m-Dollar 'Dartboard,'" *Manchester Evening News*, July 6, 1979, 1; "Masterpiece on Remand Home Wall," *London Daily Telegraph*, July 7, 1979, 17; Stanley Goldsmith, "Million Dollar Painting Found in Remand Home," *Manchester Daily Telegraph*, July 7, 1979. The *Daily Telegraph* was copublished in London and Manchester. Another daily newspaper copublished in those two cities, the *Guardian*, did not carry the story at that time. The two *Times* newspapers of London were then shut down by a prolonged strike. I owe the two Manchester newspaper references to Eleanor Jones Harvey.

19. Rita Reif, "U.S. Painting Sold for Record $2.5 Million," *New York Times*, October 26, 1979, A1, C22. Many postsale press reports, including that in the *Times*, carried a photograph of the picture, as, subsequently, did *The New York Times Index 1979: A Book of Record* (New York: *The New York Times*, 1980), 74. See also, e.g., Mark Stevens et al., "Art: A $2.5 Million Find," *Newsweek*, November 5, 1979, 115, 117; Terry Trucco, "The Art Market: Riding the Crest," *Art News* 79 (April 1980): 170; Michael Ennis, "Would You Pay $2.5 Million for That Painting?" *Texas Monthly* 8 (April 1980): 106–9, 196–200.

20. John Wilmerding et al., *American Light: The Luminist Movement, 1850–1875* (Washington, D.C.: National Gallery of Art, 1980).

21. Gerald L. Carr, essay by David C. Huntington, *Frederic Edwin Church: Catalogue Raisonné of Works of Art at Olana State Historic Site*, 2 vols. (New York and Cambridge: Cambridge University Press, 1994).

22. See n. 4.

23. Especially my *Olana Landscapes: The World of Frederic E. Church* (New York: Rizzoli International, 1989).

The artist applied the finishing touches to his masterful presentation in the accompanying broadside (fig. 16). That text is reprinted here in full for the first time. Each paragraph is paired with the corresponding details of the painting, to provide a simulacrum of the original viewers' experience of *The Icebergs.*

FIG. 16
The North. Painted by F. E. Church, from Studies of Icebergs made in the Northern Seas, in the Summer of 1859, 1862.

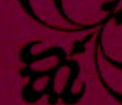
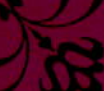

THE NORTH.

Painted by F. E. CHURCH, from Studies of Icebergs made in the Northern Seas, in the Summer of 1859.

I. THE FORM OF THE ICEBERG.

The spectator is supposed to be standing on the ice, in a bay of the berg. The several masses are parts of one immense berg. Imagine an amphitheatre, upon the lower steps of which you stand, and see the icy foreground at your feet, and gaze upon the surrounding masses, all uniting in one beneath the surface of the sea. To the left is overhanging, precipitous ice; to the right is a part of the upper surface of the berg. To that succeeds an inner gorge, running up between Alpine peaks. In front is the main portion of the berg, exhibiting ice-architecture in its vaster proportions. Thus the beholder has around him the manifold forms of the huge Greenland glacier after it has been launched upon the deep, and subjected, for a time, to the action of the elements — waves and currents, sunshine and storm.

II. MOTION OF THE ICEBERG.

Every falling mass disturbs the exact balance of the berg upon its centre, far down in the sea. Large portions are supposed to have fallen, recently, from the side on which the spectator stands, giving preponderance to the opposite side. That has gone down; this has risen. All the foreground has risen out of the waves — the arch with its bridge and bowlder, and the lower part of the great central mass, as appears from the elevation and slant of the older water-lines.

III. SURFACE OF THE ICEBERG.

A berg does not break from its own weight, but explodes from the absorption of heat, and thaws and wears away. This affords every variety of surface. On the cliffs, to the left, is a fracture, fresh and sharp, cutting like newly-broken porcelain or glass. On the right are surfaces rounded and polished by the weather. In the foreground and arch are seen the effects of the surf and currents. Upon the central mass, in front, all varieties of surface are exhibited.

IV. COLORS OF THE ICEBERG.

With the exception of an occasional vein, which is blue as sapphire, or stains from rock, an iceberg is purely white, an opaque, dead white,— ghastly and spiritless in a dull atmosphere; but in bright weather, especially late in the afternoon, kindling with a varied splendor. The picture aims to represent the berg at that brilliant hour. Lights and shadows, hues and tints, shower the scene, and are thrown in all ways, and multiplied by reflection. The pale-blue bands, on the left, are the veins alluded to,— simply clear, transparent ice, formed in the cracks of the glacier. All the darker blues are only white ice under shadows. The green ice, as in the arch, is only green by reflection of the green water.

V. THE SEA.

From the brightness of an iceberg the eye is so affected that the sea appears very dark. Accordingly the beholder here looks out through a gradually widening avenue to the broad water, and finds it a very dark purple or violet. The sea, close in, partakes, with the surrounding ice, of all the brilliant reflections. Where the sea comes in contact with ice it is a lively green. Hence the emerald water of the foreground, and at the base of the great central mass. The pale-blue water just below the spectator, on the foreground, is an example of the pools of fresh water on the top of icebergs.

VI. THE SKY.

From the same optical causes that the sea is dark, the sky is sombre, rather than of a luminous azure. Fog, a feature of icebergs, is sweeping the heights in front, and reddening in the late afternoon light.

VII. EXPRESSION OF THE SCENE.

All things favoring, an iceberg, in itself alone, is a miracle of beauty and grandeur. A fine, quiet afternoon at sea affords all the requisites. Hence the picture presents the beholder with ice only, reposing, under the brightness of the declining sun, in the calm, solitary ocean,— grandeur with repose. The flight of the mist is noiseless. The swells come gently rolling in, in glassy circles, breaking with low murmur on the icy foreground.

On Exhibition at the BOSTON ATHENÆUM, Beacon Street.

Prentiss & Deland, Printers, 40, Congress Street.

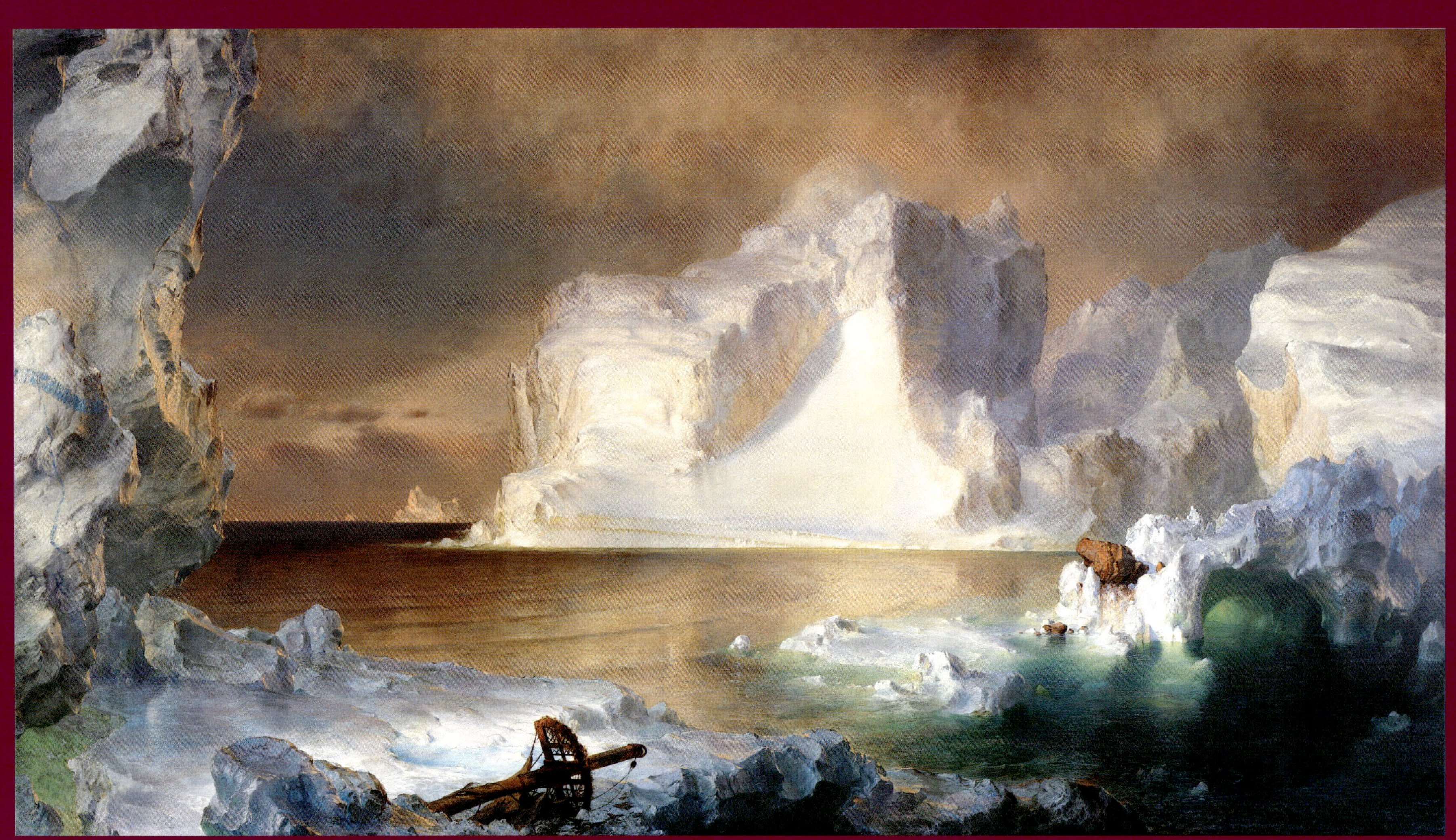

I. The Form of the Iceberg.

The spectator is supposed to be standing on the ice, in a bay of the berg. The several masses are parts of one immense berg. Imagine an amphitheatre, upon the lower steps of which you stand, and see the icy foreground at your feet, and gaze upon the surrounding masses, all uniting in one beneath the surface of the sea. To the left is overhanging, precipitous ice; to the right is a part of the upper surface of the berg. To that succeeds an inner gorge, running up between Alpine peaks. In front is the main portion of the berg, exhibiting ice-architecture in its vaster proportions. Thus the beholder has around him the manifold forms of the huge Greenland glacier after it has been launched upon the deep, and subjected, for a time, to the action of the elements—waves and currents, sunshine and storm.

II. Motion of the Iceberg.

Every falling mass disturbs the exact balance of the berg upon its centre, far down in the sea. Large portions are supposed to have fallen, recently, from the side on which the spectator stands, giving preponderance to the opposite side. That has gone down; this has risen. All the foreground has risen out of the waves—the arch with its bridge and bowlder, and the lower part of the great central mass, as appears from the elevation and slant of the older water-lines.

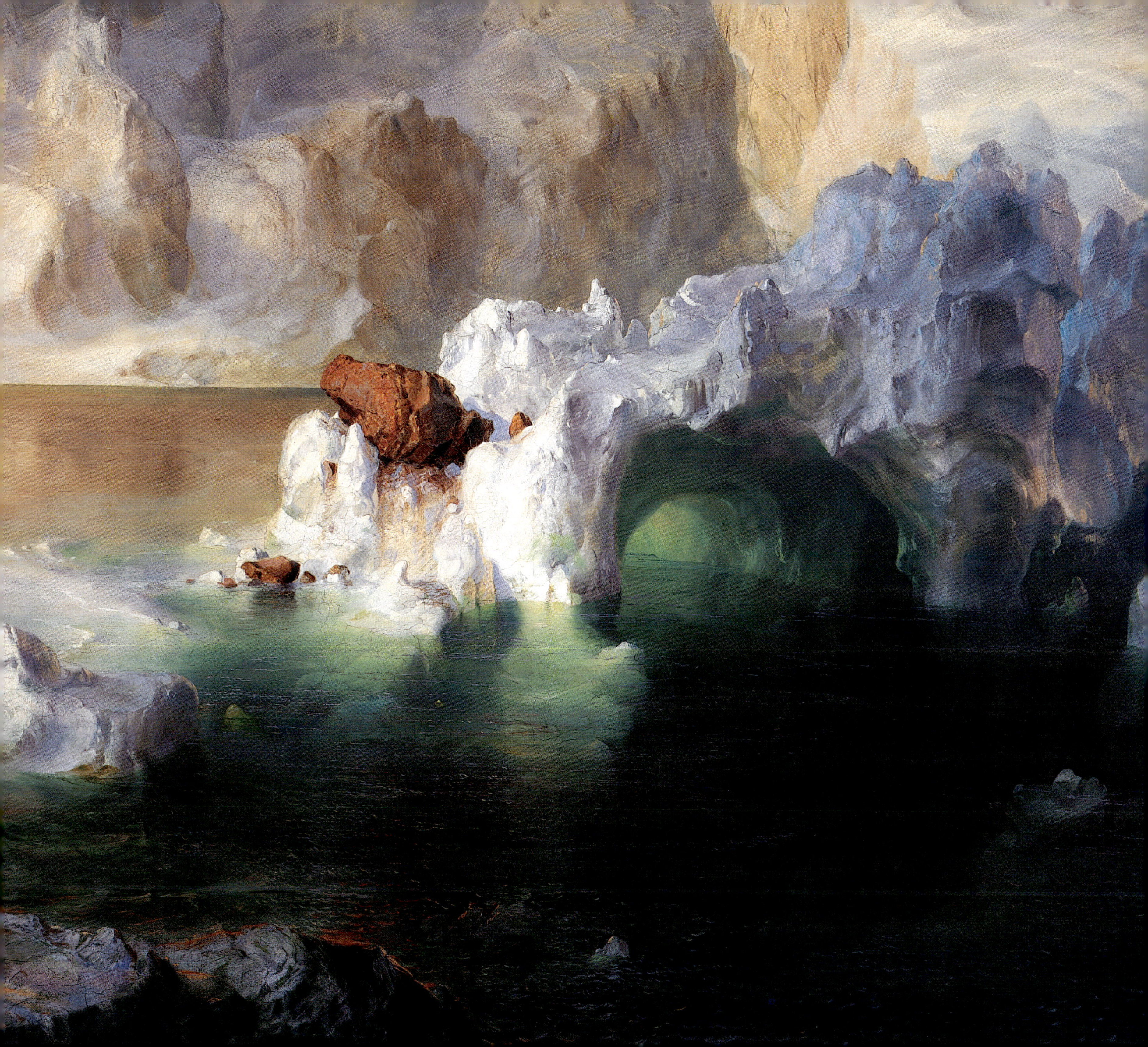

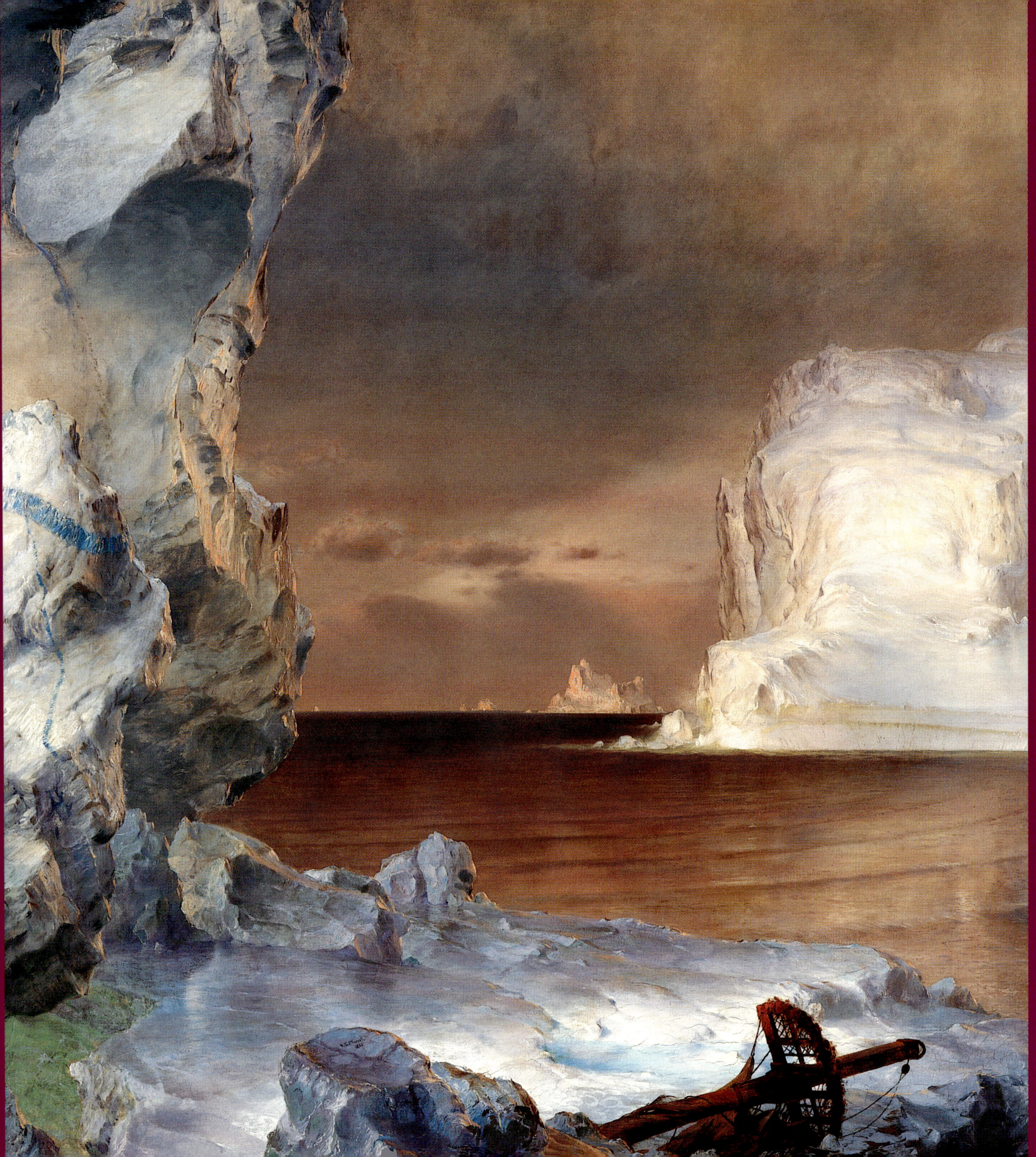

III. Surface of the Iceberg.

A berg does not break from its own weight, but explodes from the absorption of heat, and thaws and wears away. This affords every variety of surface. On the cliffs, to the left, is a fracture, fresh and sharp, cutting like newly-broken porcelain or glass. On the right are surfaces rounded and polished by the weather. In the foreground and arch are seen the effects of the surf and currents. Upon the central mass, in front, all varieties of surface are exhibited.

IV. Colors of the Iceberg.

With the exception of an occasional vein, which is blue as sapphire, or stains from rock, an iceberg is purely white, an opaque, dead white,—ghastly and spiritless in a dull atmosphere; but in bright weather, especially late in the afternoon, kindling with a varied splendor. The picture aims to represent the berg at that brilliant hour. Lights and shadows, hues and tints, shower the scene, and are thrown in all ways, and multiplied by reflection. The pale-blue bands, on the left, are the veins alluded to,—simply clear, transparent ice, formed in the cracks of the glacier. All the darker blues are only white ice under shadows. The green ice, as in the arch, is only green by reflection of the green water.

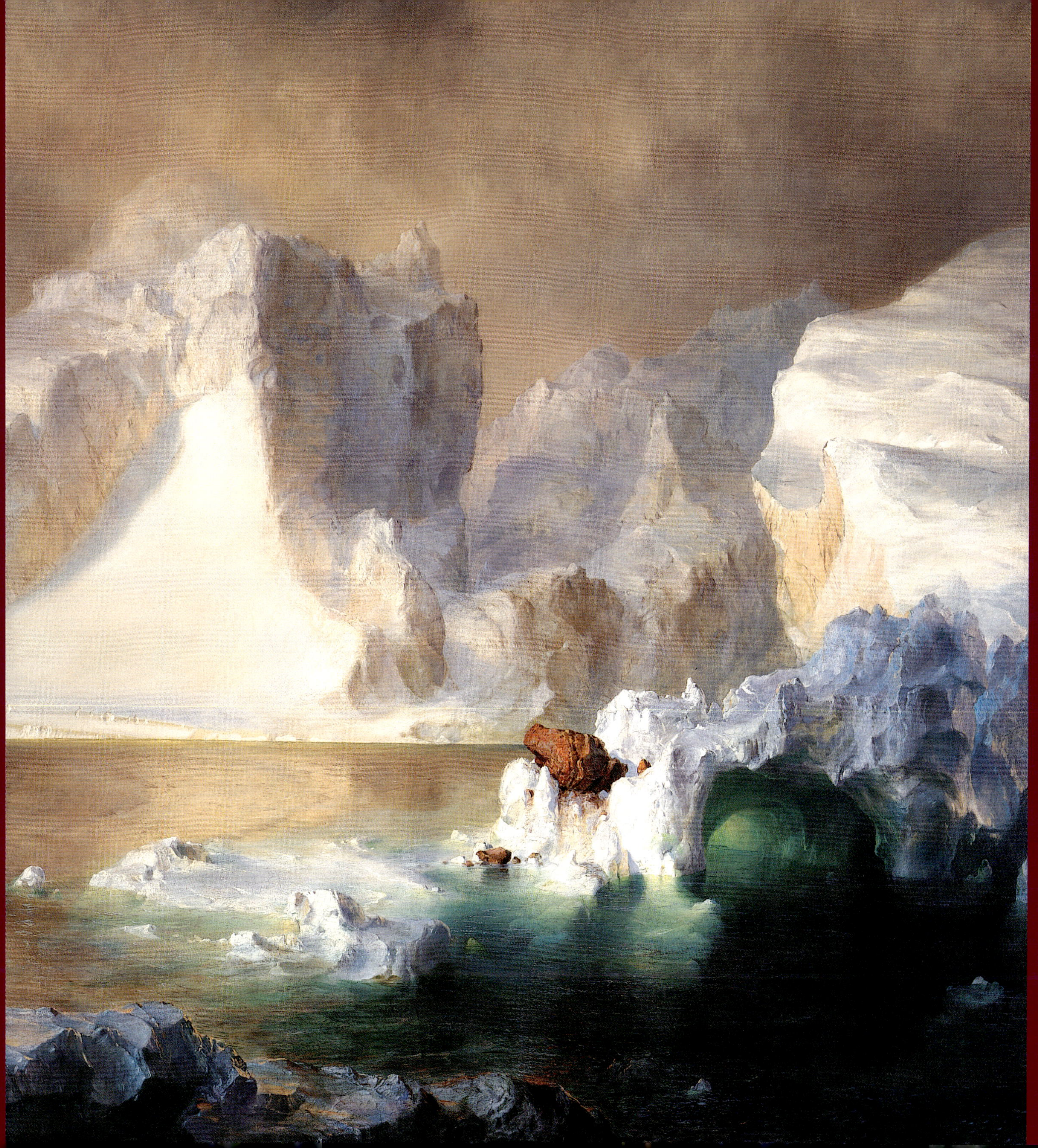

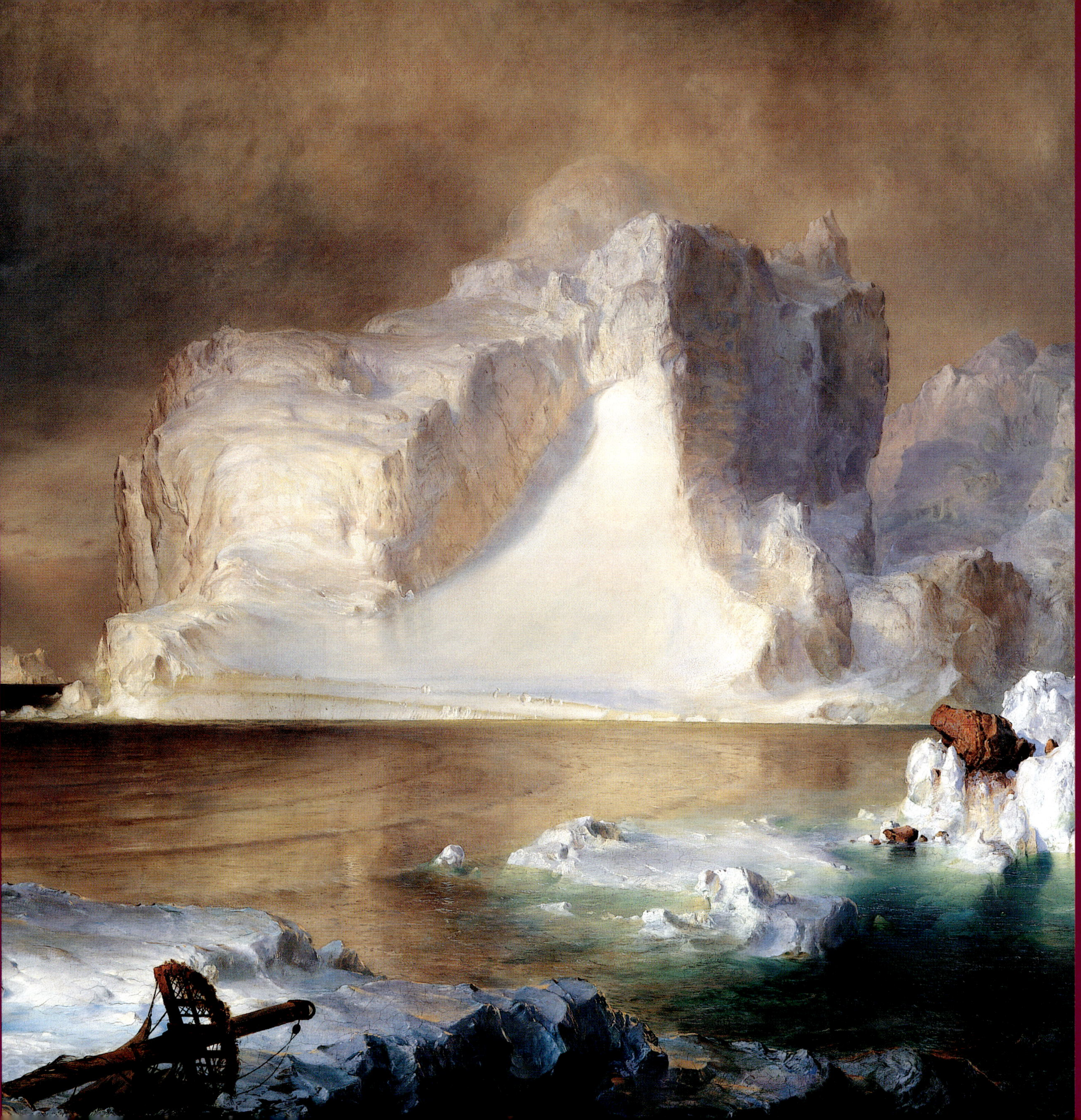

V. The Sea.

From the brightness of an iceberg the eye is so affected that the sea appears very dark. Accordingly the beholder here looks out through a gradually widening avenue to the broad water, and finds it a very dark purple or violet. The sea, close in, partakes, with the surrounding ice, of all the brilliant reflections. Where the sea comes in contact with ice it is a lively green. Hence the emerald water of the foreground, and at the base of the great central mass. The pale-blue water just below the spectator, on the foreground, is an example of the pools of fresh water on the top of icebergs.

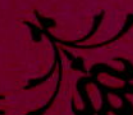

VI. The Sky.

From the same optical causes that the sea is dark, the sky is sombre, rather than of a luminous azure. Fog, a feature of icebergs, is sweeping the heights in front, and reddening in the late afternoon light.

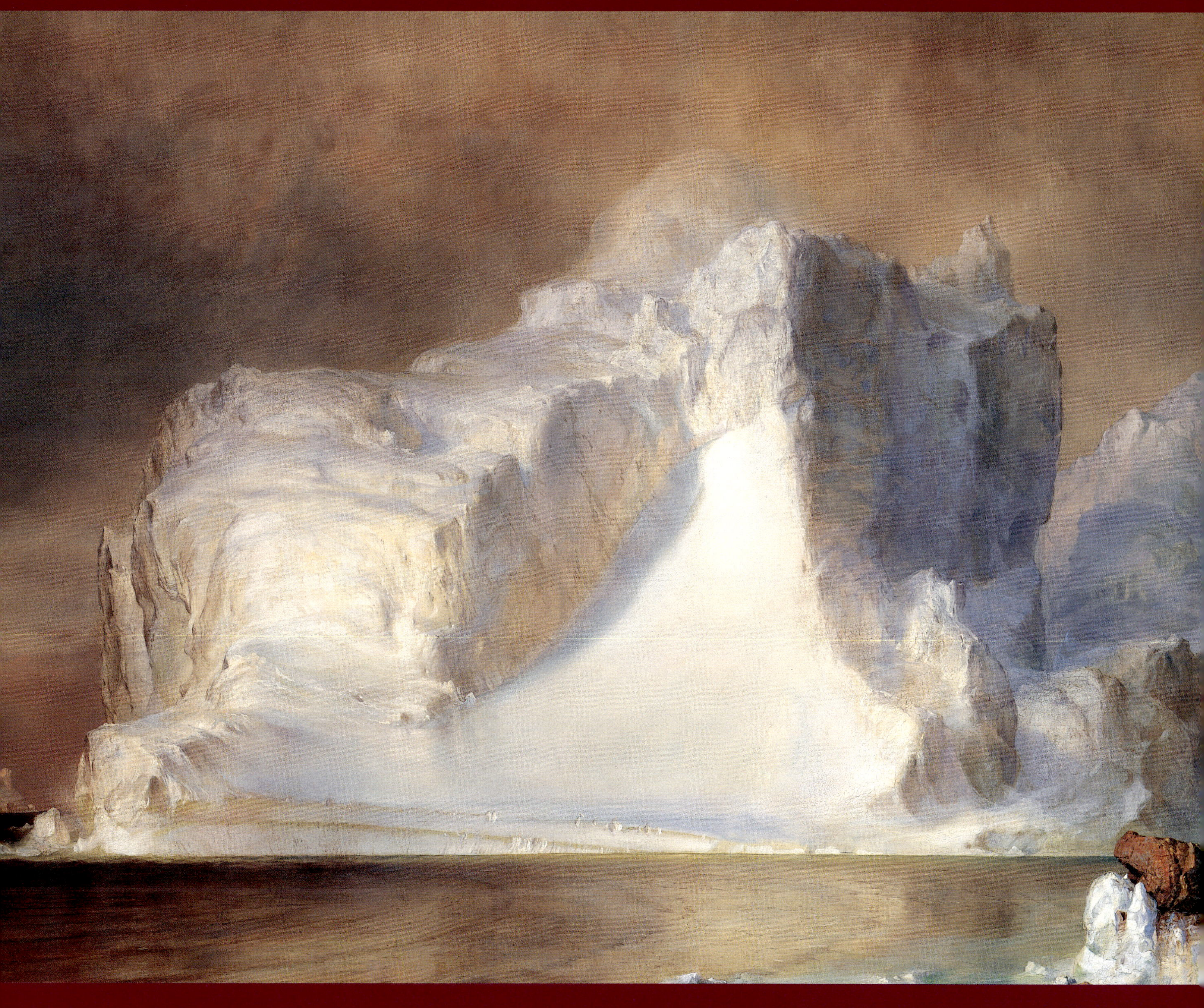

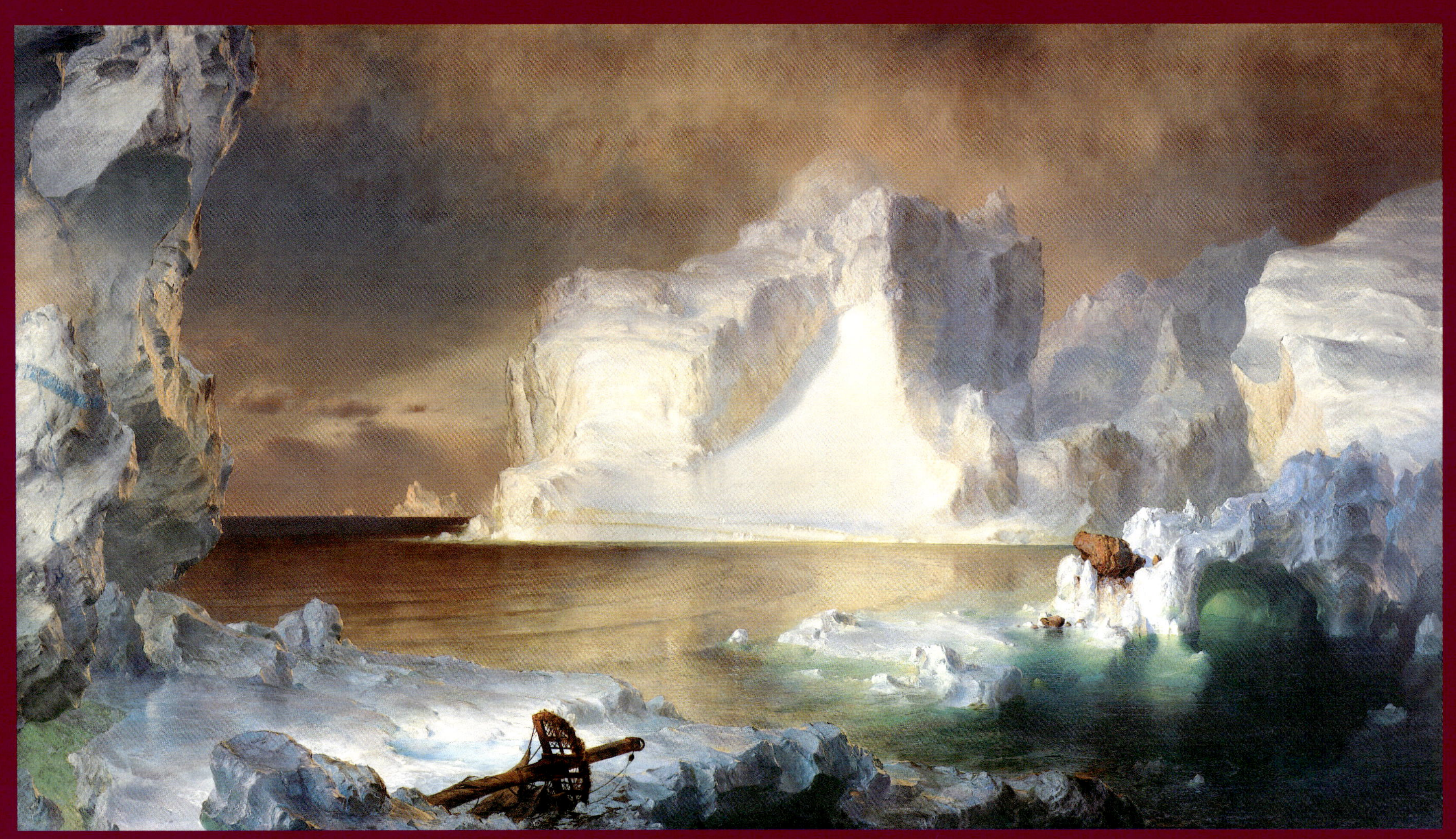

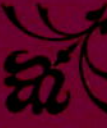

VII. Expression of the Scene.

All things favoring, an iceberg, in itself alone, is a miracle of beauty and grandeur. A fine, quiet afternoon at sea affords all the requisites. Hence the picture presents the beholder with ice only, reposing, under the brightness of the declining sun, in the calm, solitary ocean,—grandeur with repose. The flight of the mist is noiseless. The swells come gently rolling in, in glassy circles, breaking with low murmur on the icy foreground.

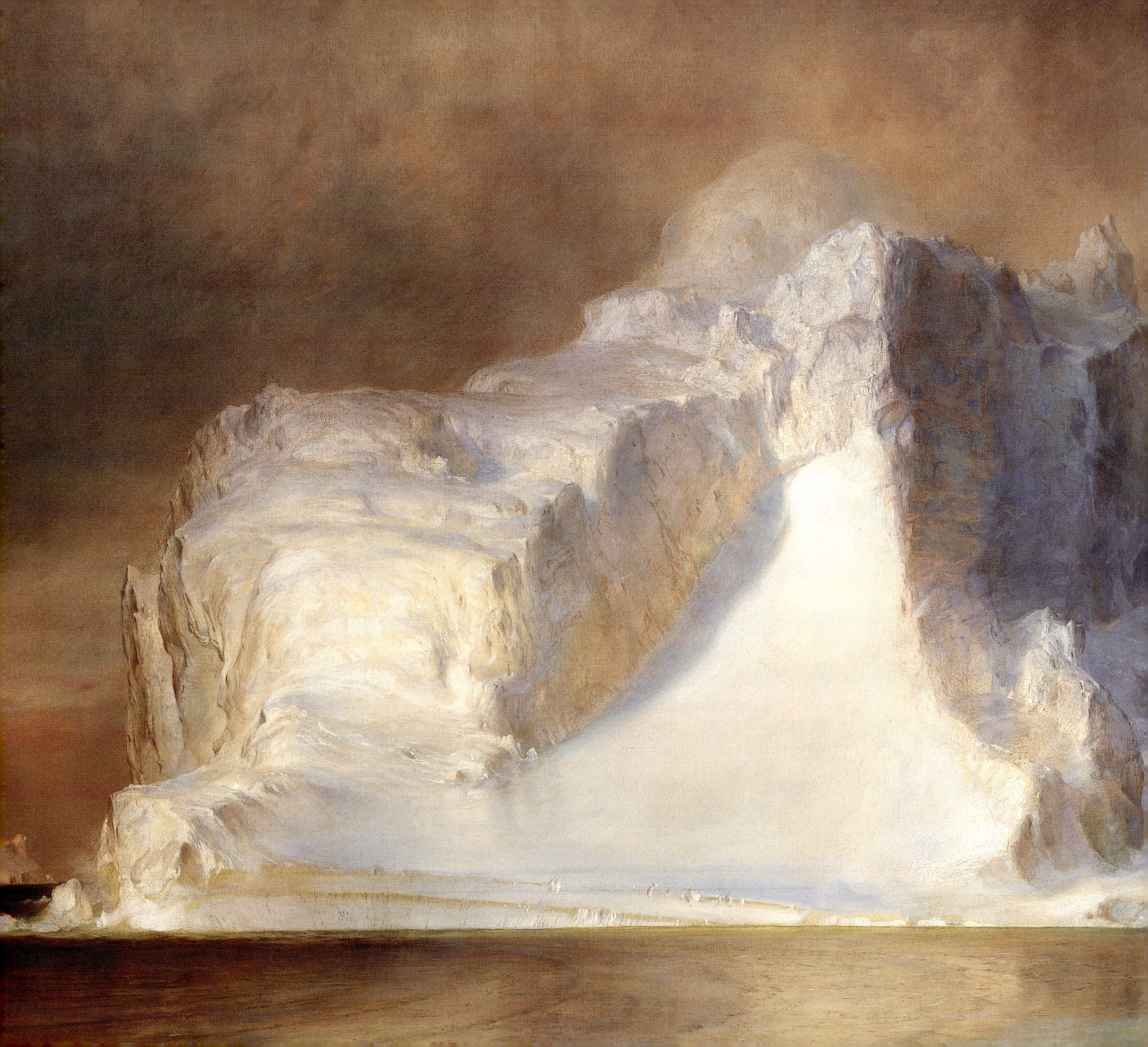

Eleanor Jones Harvey

THE TIP OF *The Icebergs*

In May 1862 Frederic Edwin Church had a problem. His latest "Great Picture," a six-by-nine-foot canvas called *The North*—now known as *The Icebergs*—had failed to find a buyer, after being shown first in New York and then in Boston. As he had done with great success before, Church had carefully orchestrated the advance publicity surrounding this newest work: the painting made its debut at Goupil's Gallery in New York City and garnered lengthy and glowing reports in the press. For *The North*, as with *Niagara* in 1857 (fig. 5) and *The Heart of the Andes* in 1859 (fig. 6), Church charged admission for the privilege of viewing his latest "Great Picture" and published a broadside that would enhance the visitors' experience. This marketing strategy, popularized in Great Britain and admirably adapted by Church, had worked splendidly before. But now, facing an unsold painting that was a year old, Church had to confront what had gone wrong and find a permanent home for his first marketing failure.

The "Great Picture" stratagem used the twin engines of publicity and exclusivity to attract notice to a (usually large-scale) painting. For Church, this meant scheduling a solo exhibition for each successive painting in New York, usually coinciding with the annual group exhibition at the National Academy of Design (NAD). Although Church was a member of the NAD, he rarely sent the academy his grandest work; instead, he used his studio or one of the newly emergent commercial galleries as an exhibition venue and created a singular moment for each of his paintings. After exhibition in New York, *Niagara* and *The Heart of the Andes* had both been shown in London, again to high

(DETAIL)
Frederic Edwin Church,
The Icebergs, 1861.
Oil on canvas, 64½ × 112½ in.
Dallas Museum of Art, Anonymous gift, 1979.28.

praise,[1] and both paintings had sold for record prices—information that was also widely publicized. In this manner Church built an audience that waited with anticipation for his next great unveiling. The press did its part, reporting on the artist's summer sketching trips, guessing what the next subject might be. Church's literary friends provided a pamphlet extolling *Niagara* and a pair of essays for *The Heart of the Andes*, to ease the viewer's absorption into the visual spectacle.[2] However, in the case of *The North*, all such efforts had failed to accomplish the desired result: a buyer and possibly another record-setting price for his—or any other American artist's—paintings. To complicate matters further, Church had other paintings under way, making *The Icebergs* an unexpected presence in his Tenth Street studio.

Church was at the top of his form in 1861, when he painted *The Icebergs*.[3] Church was a precocious and talented landscape painter for whom success seemed to come naturally. Elected a full academician of the NAD in 1849, at twenty-three, he was the youngest artist so honored. Accolades for his earlier "Great Pictures" set high expectations when the news leaked out in 1859 that Church was headed north, to Labrador, that summer to sketch icebergs in the southern Arctic region. He took with him Louis Legrand Noble, a prominent friend who had been Thomas Cole's pastor and eulogist. Noble's function was to observe Church at work, record their adventures, and present them in a book-length narrative to be published just prior to the debut of Church's Arctic "Great Picture." It was a carefully calibrated exercise in marketing that was as deftly crafted as the painting.

Church's interest in the Arctic was shared by a broad audience captivated by the saga of the Franklin Expedition, presumed lost after disappearing into the Canadian Arctic in 1845. When the British Royal Navy reluctantly announced that Franklin and his two ships were still missing in 1847, the news spurred numerous search efforts, most of them sponsored in Britain and America. Over the next few decades, some fifty ships sailed into Hudson Bay in an effort first to find Franklin, then to discover the remains of his expedition, and finally to reach the North Pole or attempt to navigate a Northwest Passage. The search for Franklin had all the earmarks of a valiant rescue and a romantic quest for personal and national acclaim in a region presenting a frontier of unknown proportions and chilling prospects, literally and psychologically.[4]

In June 1859 Church and Noble took the steamship *Merlin* on one of its regular runs from Halifax, Nova Scotia, to St. John's, Newfoundland, and from there chartered the schooner *Integrity* to bring them closer to the ice floes.[5] While on board the *Integrity*'s rowboat, Church sketched their quarry as the small craft lurched from the sea's motion. Noble did not lack for colorful anecdotes. In addition to his evocative descriptions of the icebergs themselves, he composed vignettes describing the artist at work, designed to permit his homebound audience to understand the queasiness Church felt as he sketched the icebergs in less than calm seas. While Church battled seasickness, Noble observed, "If one is curious about the troubles of painting on a little coaster, lightly ballasted, dashing forward frequently under a press of sail, with a short sea, I would recommend him to a good

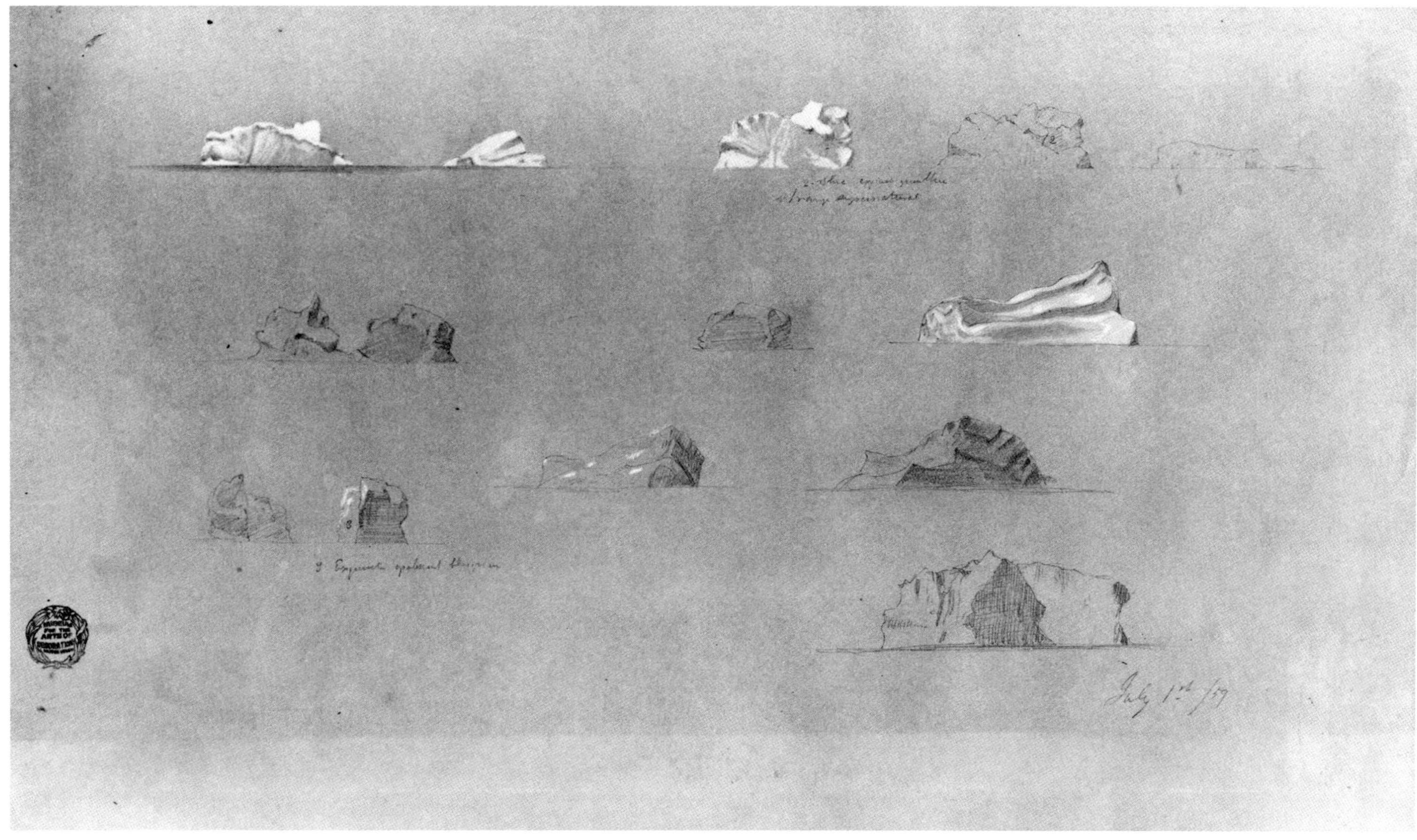

stout swing. While in the enjoyment of his smooth and sickening vibrations, let him spread his pallet [*sic*], arrange his canvas, and paint a pair of colts at their gambols in some adjacent field."[6] Paired with the sketches in pencil and oil that Church brought back from that summer, Noble's narrative, published in 1861, presented an illustrated travelogue designed to familiarize his readers with an environment far more alien than the Andean plateau featured in Church's last "Great Picture."

Some of Church's sketches are little more than deft pencilings annotated with his numerical color shorthand; others are far more detailed. On a page dated July 1, 1859 (fig. 17), the artist's notations include "exquisite opalescent blue-green" and "Strange, supernatural." Noble reveled in the range of descriptive adjectives the two men brought to bear on the optical effects on the ice:

> In the seams and fissures the shadows are the softest blue of the skies, and as plain and palpable as smoke. It melts at every pore, and streams as if a perpetually overflowing fountain

FIG. 17

Frederic Edwin Church, ***Icebergs***, July 1, 1859.
Graphite, brush and white gouache on green wove paper, 10¾ × 17⅞ in.
Cooper-Hewitt, National Design Museum, Smithsonian Institution/Art Resource, NY, Gift of Louis P. Church, 1917-4-298. Photo: Scott Hyde.

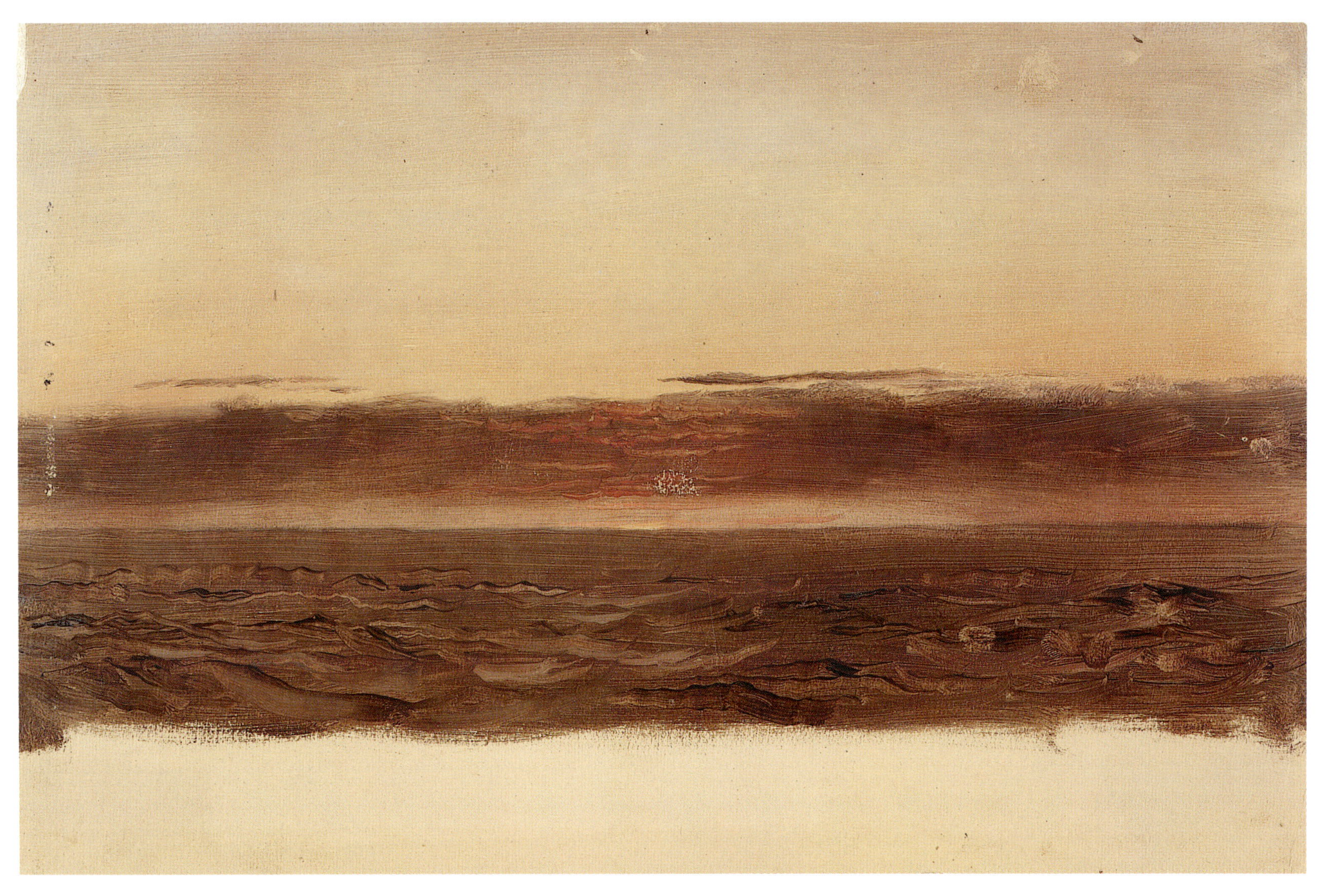

FIG. 18
Frederic Edwin Church, ***Labrador (Seascape)***,
June–July 1859.
Oil and graphite on paper, 8 × 11$^{13}/_{16}$ in.
Cooper-Hewitt, National Design Museum, Smithsonian Institution/Art Resource, NY, Gift of Louis P. Church, 1917-4-818. Photo: Matt Flynn.

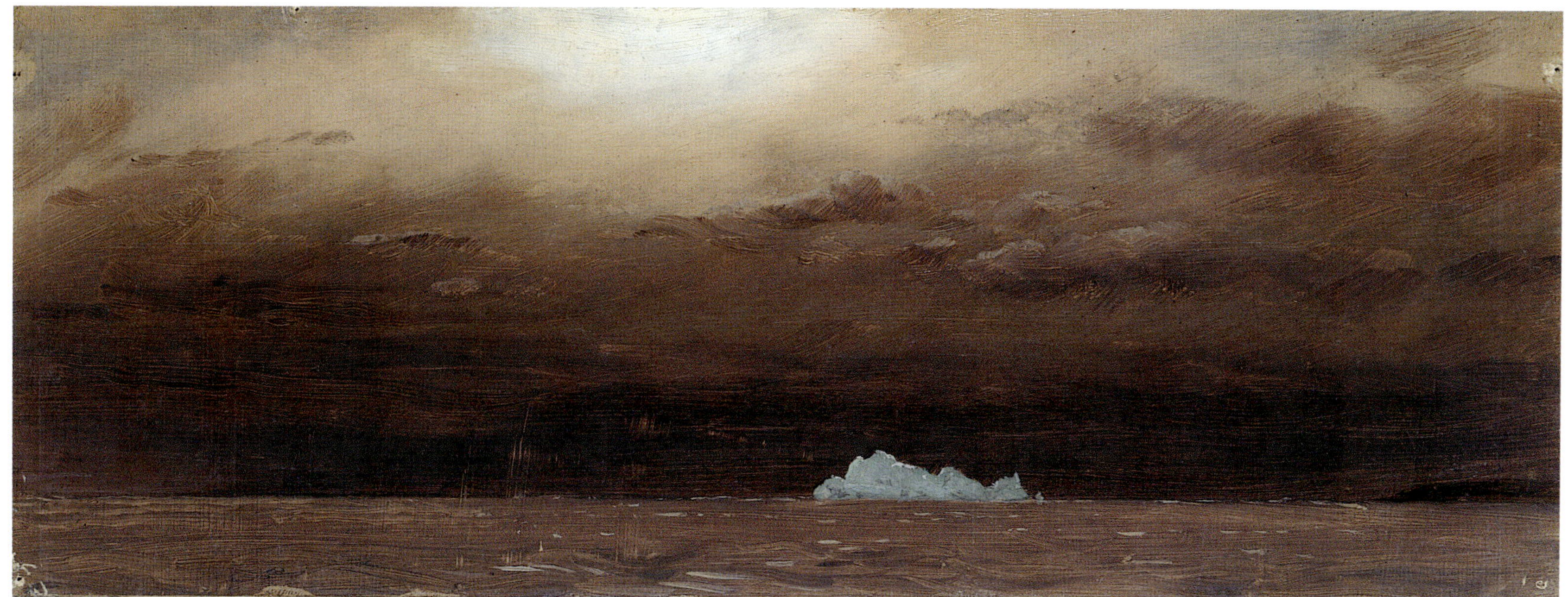

FIG. 19
Frederic Edwin Church, ***Iceberg, Newfoundland,*** June 1859.
Oil and traces of graphite on thin paperboard, 5⅜ × 14⅞ in. Cooper-Hewitt, National Design Museum, Smithsonian Institution/Art Resource, NY, Gift of Louis P. Church, 1917-4-296-c. Photo: Matt Flynn.

> were upon the summit, and flashes and scintillates like one vast brilliant. Prongs and reefs of ice jutting from the body of the berg below, and over which we pass, give the water that emerald clearness so lovely to the eye, and open to view something like the fanciful sea-green caves.[7]

Spending anywhere from a few minutes to several hours on a single sheet, Church painted a series of oil sketches of an advancing iceberg framed by the dark ocean. Although they are undated, they read sequentially, beginning with a long, narrow rectangle dominated by a vacant sea, the strips of water and sky rendered in broad, abstract strokes. In a sketch simply titled *Labrador (Seascape)* (fig. 18), a nearly imperceptible whiteness on the horizon heralds the first sighting of the iceberg. The sheets are soon filled with diminutive white forms on the horizon, the icebergs small against the vastness of the ocean and sky. At least six more panoramic oil sketches of individual bergs emphasize their mass as they loom tall above the waterline, finally filling the entire sheet (figs. 19–24). In such sketches as *Floating Iceberg* (fig. 25), Church lavished attention on his detailed articulation of the icy surfaces, his rendering achieving architectonic strength, the bergs' solid forms standing out against the more fluid, abstract expanses of sky and water.

Church returned to New York with close to one hundred sketches in pencil and oil that would form the basis of his Arctic imagery. That winter, however, he completed *Twilight in the Wilderness* (fig. 26), which made its debut in June 1860. Church did not return to his Arctic sketches for more

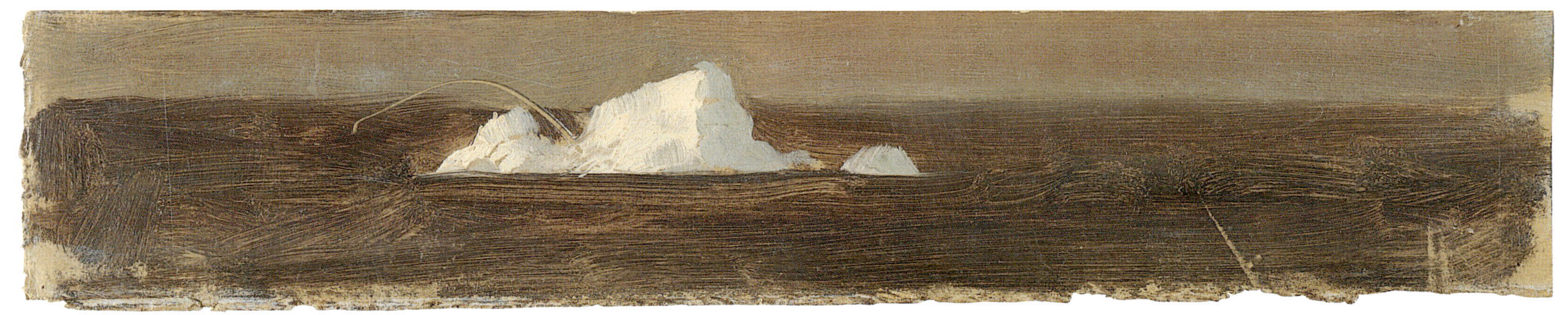

FIG. 20
Frederic Edwin Church, ***Floating Icebergs***, June–July 1859.
Oil on paperboard, 2⁵⁄₁₆ × 11⅝ in.
Cooper-Hewitt, National Design Museum, Smithsonian Institution/Art Resource, NY, Gift of Louis P. Church, 1917-4-749-b. Photo: Matt Flynn.

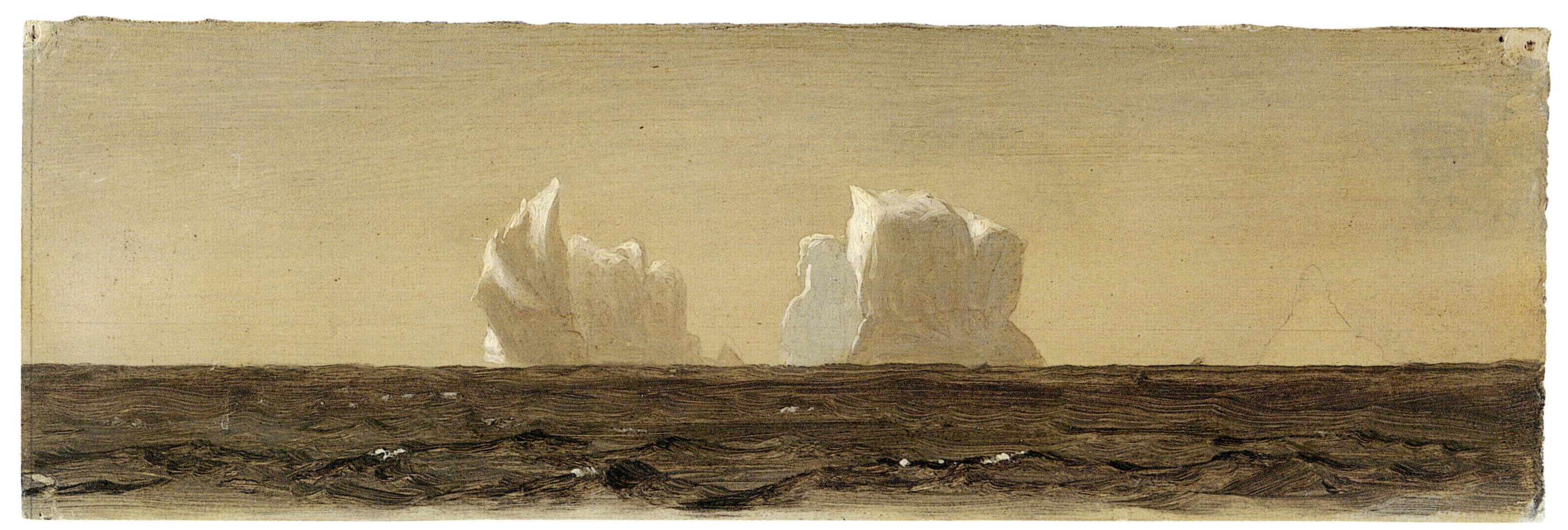

FIG. 21
Frederic Edwin Church, ***Floating Icebergs***,
June–July 1859.
Oil and graphite on paperboard, $3\frac{11}{16} \times 11\frac{1}{8}$ in.
Cooper-Hewitt, National Design Museum, Smithsonian Institution/Art Resource, NY, Gift of Louis P. Church, 1917-4-290-a. Photo: Matt Flynn.

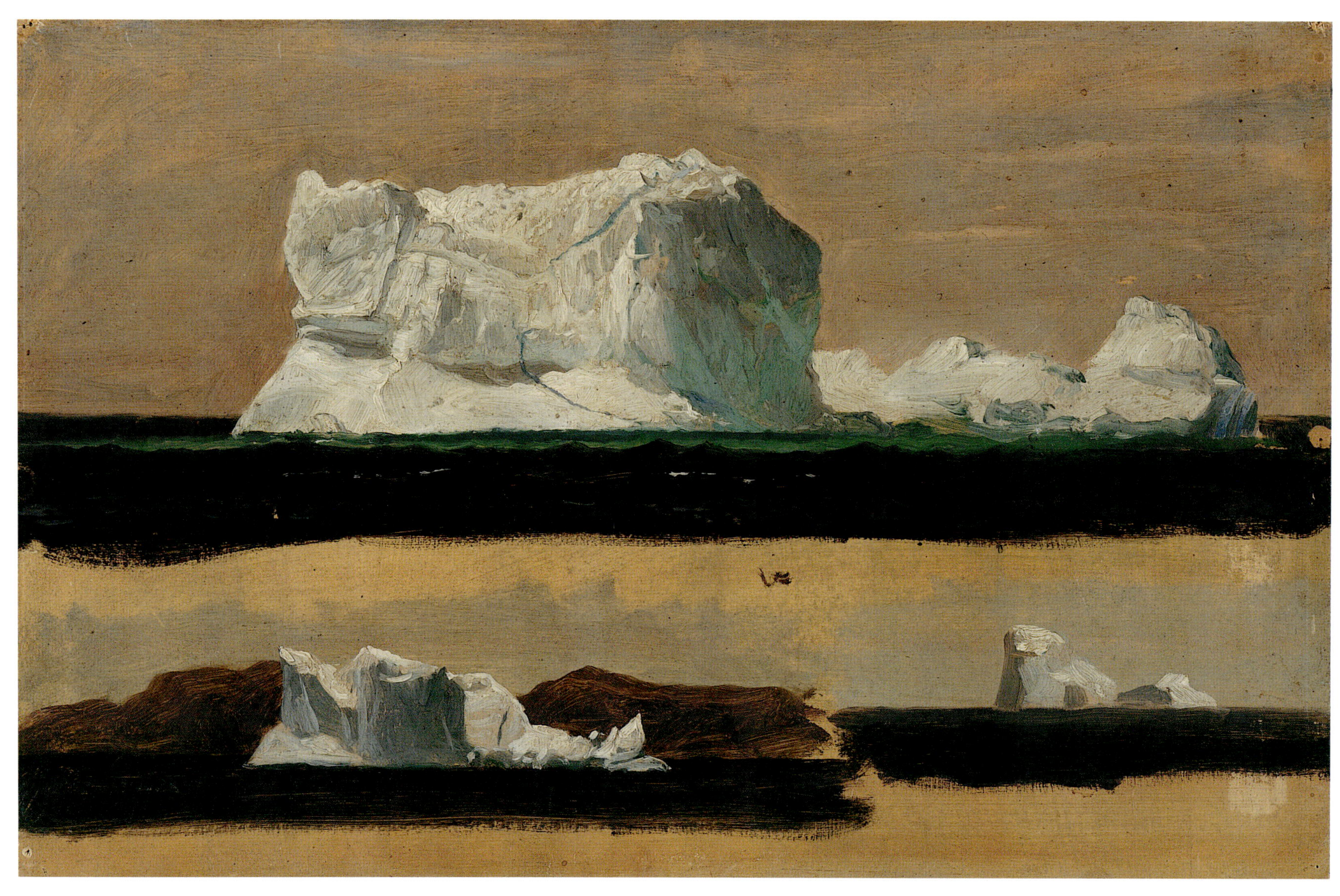

FIG. 22

Frederic Edwin Church, ***Iceberg near Twillingate, Newfoundland,*** July 1859.

Oil on thin buff paperboard, 11 15/16 × 18 1/8 in.

Cooper-Hewitt, National Design Museum, Smithsonian Institution/Art Resource, NY, Gift of Louis P. Church, 1917-4-294-a. Photo: Matt Flynn.

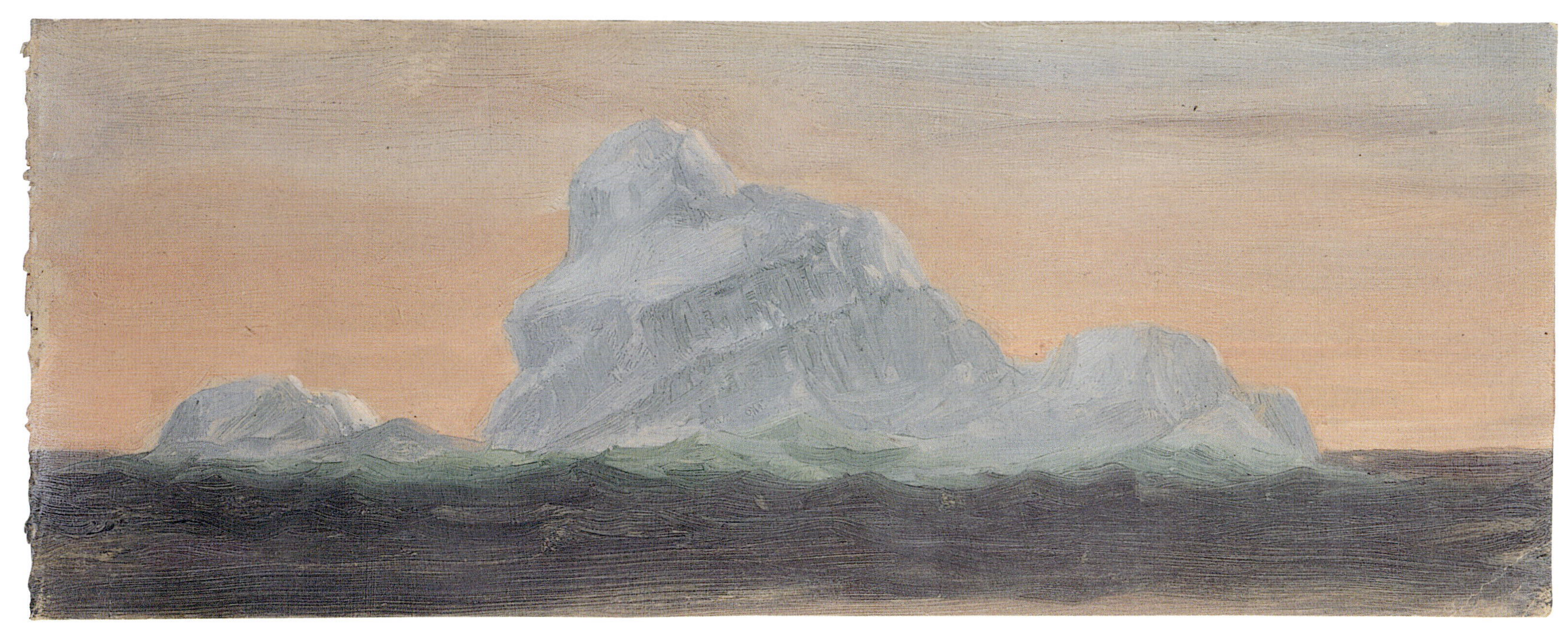

FIG. 23
Frederic Edwin Church, ***Iceberg against Evening Sky***, June–July 1859.
Oil on thin buff paperboard, 4 9/16 × 11 9/16 in.
Cooper-Hewitt, National Design Museum, Smithsonian Institution/Art Resource, NY, Gift of Louis P. Church, 1917-4-731. Photo: Matt Flynn.

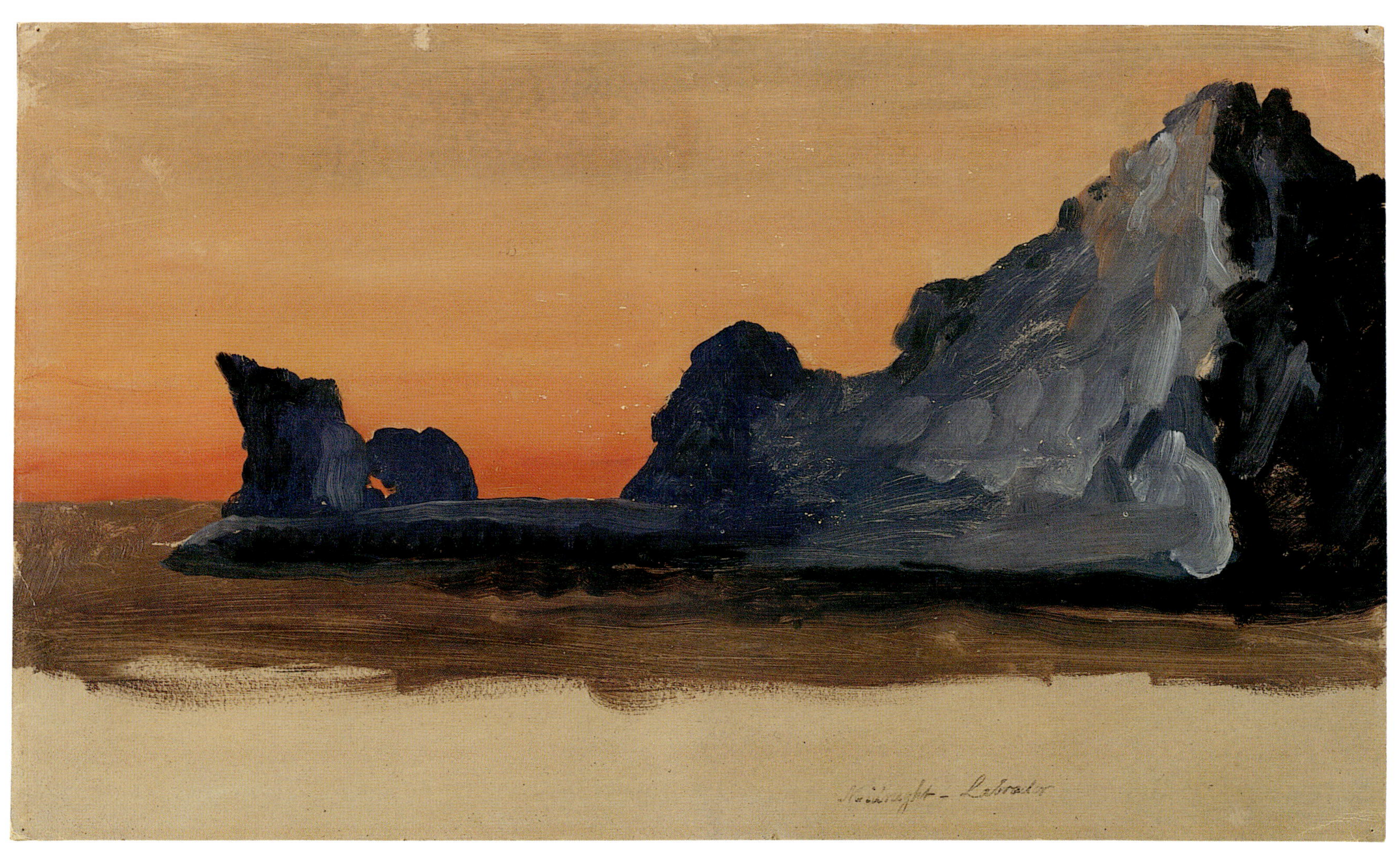

FIG. 24
Frederic Edwin Church, ***Icebergs at Midnight, Labrador,*** June–July 1859.
Oil on paperboard, 12 × 19 15/16 in.
Cooper-Hewitt, National Design Museum, Smithsonian Institution/Art Resource, NY, Gift of Louis P. Church, 1917-4-711. Photo: Matt Flynn.

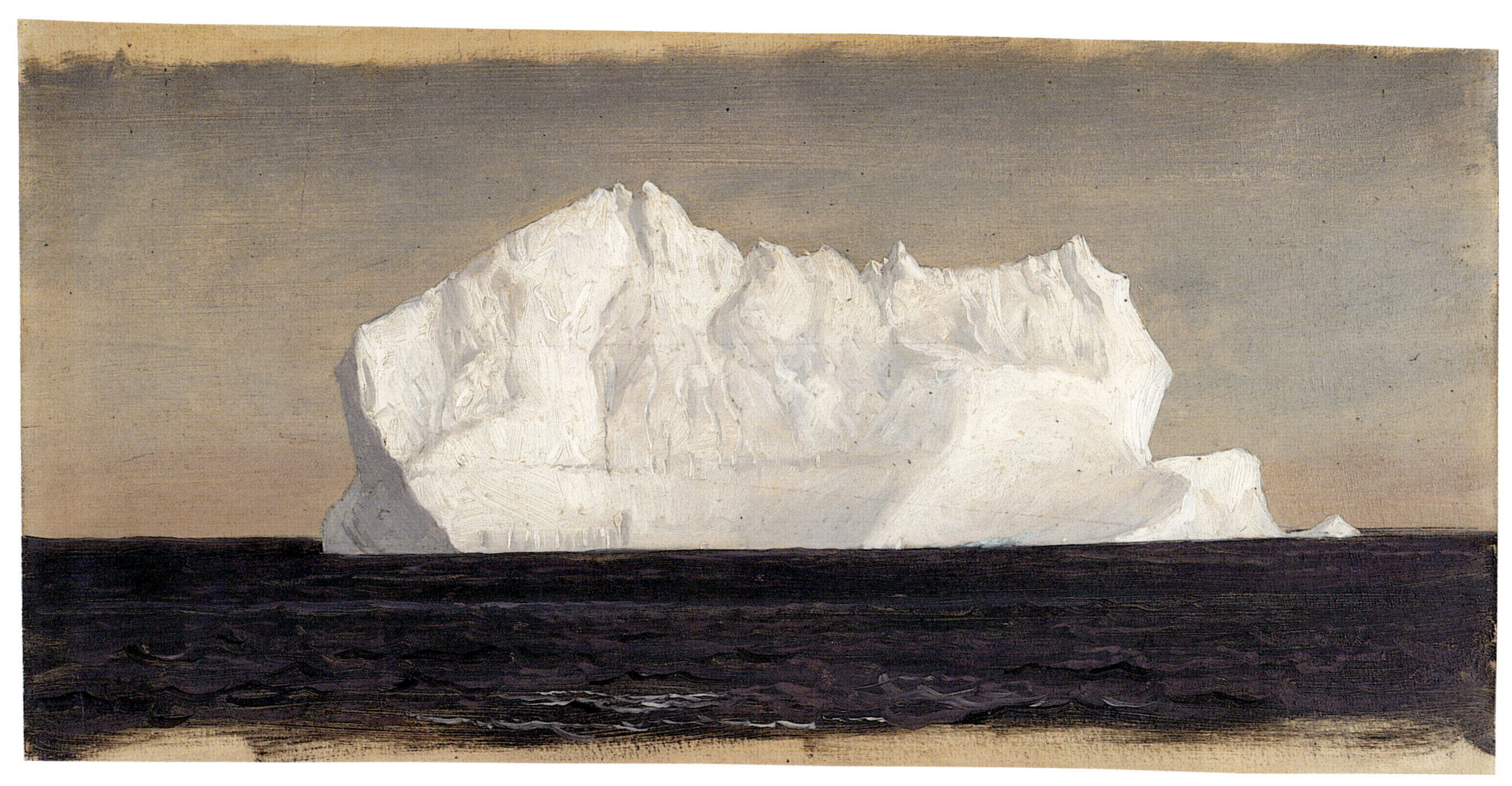

FIG. 25
Frederic Edwin Church, ***Floating Iceberg,***
June–July 1859.
Oil and graphite on thin paperboard, 7⅜ × 14$^{13}/_{16}$ in.
Cooper-Hewitt, National Design Museum, Smithsonian Institution/Art Resource, NY, Gift of Louis P. Church, 1917-4-296-a. Photo: Matt Flynn.

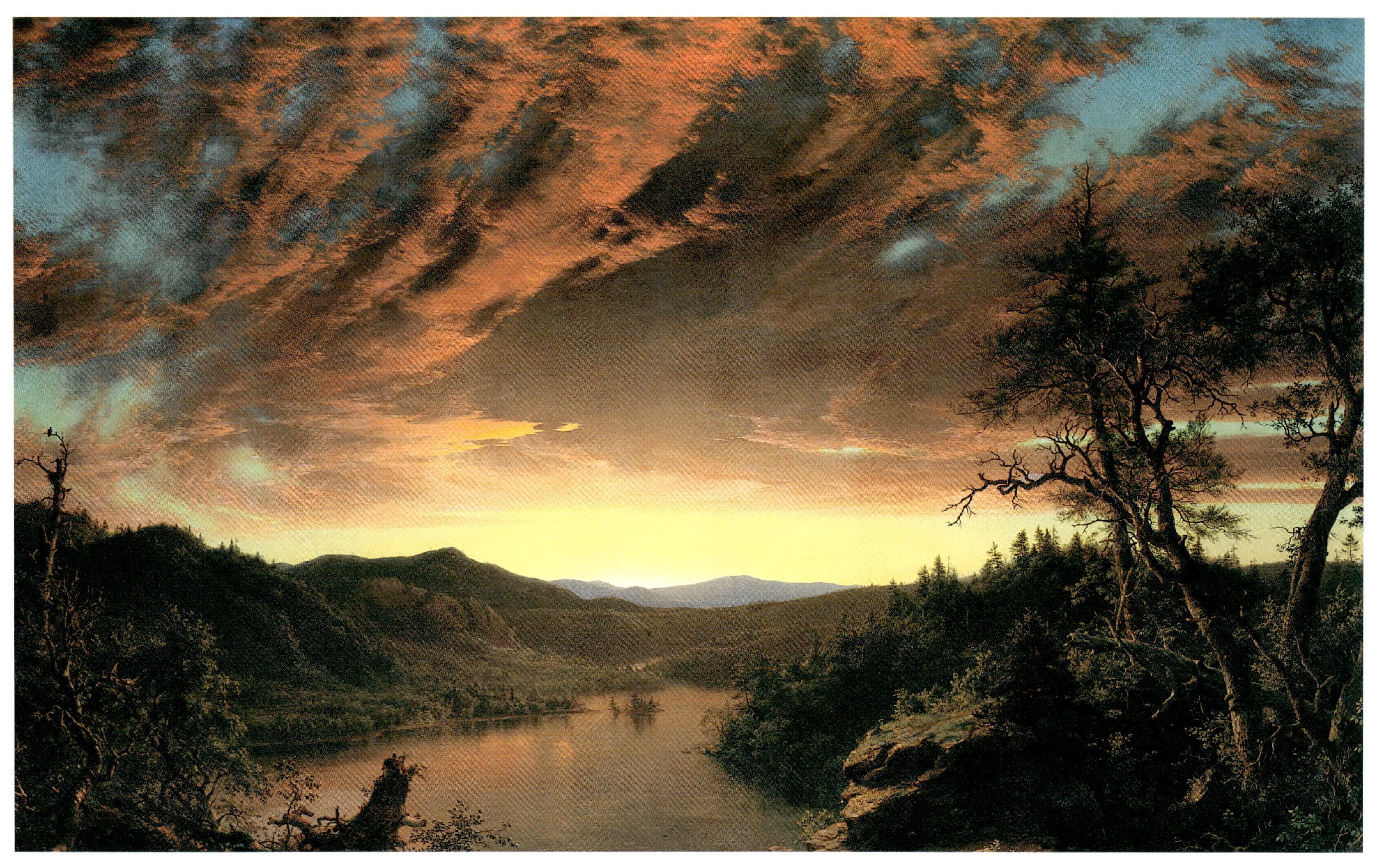

FIG. 26
Frederic Edwin Church, ***Twilight in the Wilderness***, 1860.
Oil on canvas, 40 × 64 in.
© The Cleveland Museum of Art, 2002, Mr. and Mrs. William H. Marlatt Fund, 1965.233.

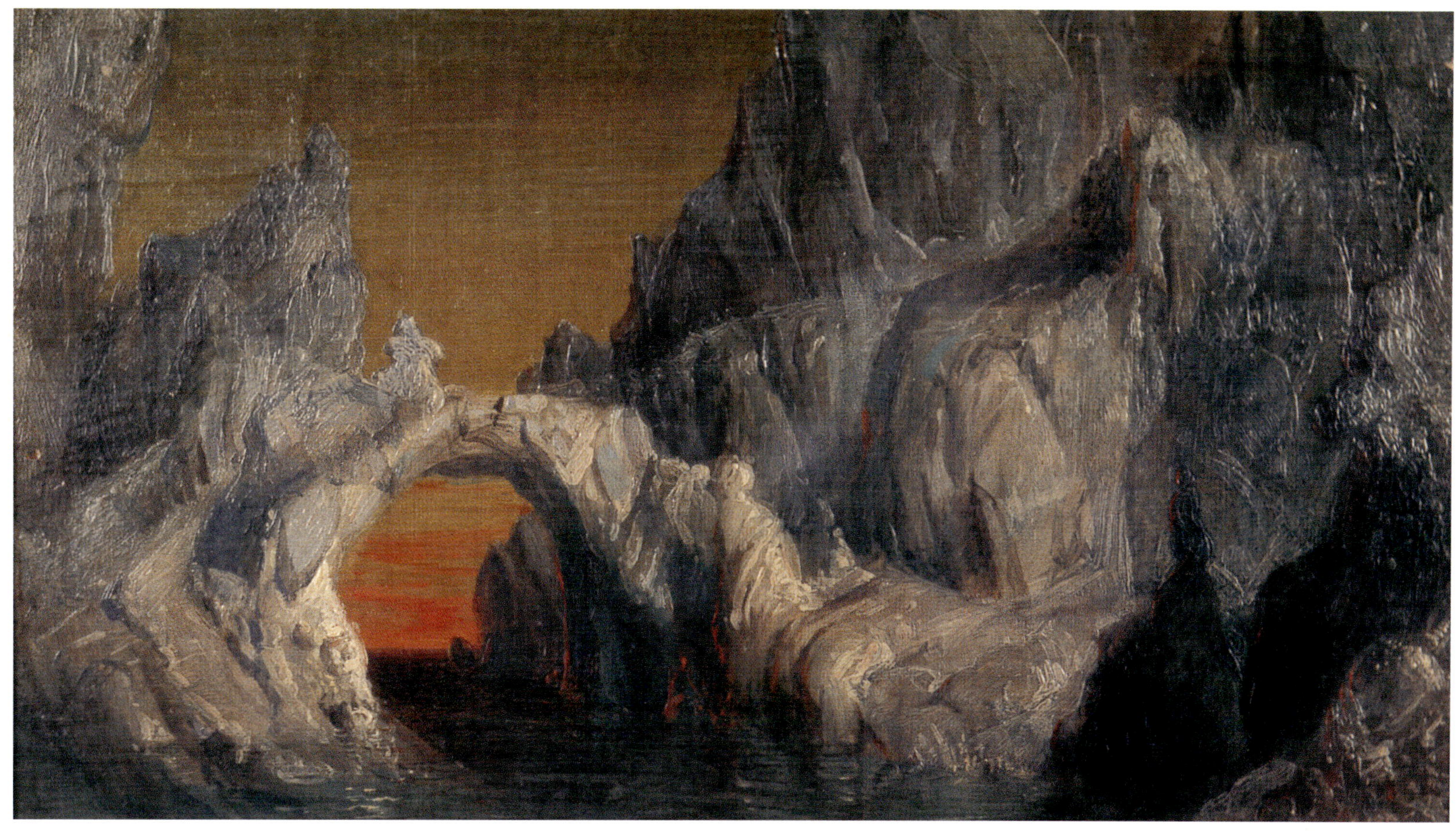

than a full year, spending the winter of 1860–61 laboring behind closed doors to complete *The Icebergs*. Prior to his travels, Church had begun studying the nature of ice and glaciation, and may well have made sketches to clarify his understanding of the northern archipelago. As he had done already with *The Heart of the Andes*, Church created the composition of *The Icebergs* as much from his imagination as his on-site sketches. His goal was to capture both the essence of his experiences among icebergs and the other-worldly sense of the Arctic environment, drawn from explorers' reports and his friendship with Dr. Isaac Hayes.

Church began by experimenting with several preliminary ideas before settling on the structural features depicted in *The Icebergs*. In one early sketch (fig. 27), Church focused on the ice cave that will eventually appear in the left foreground and the somewhat lurid tones of the summer sky. *Icebergs and Wreck in Sunset* (fig. 28) indicates that Church had considered including evidence of a shipwreck long before he added the broken mast, two years later. At some point, then, he made

FIG. 27
Frederic Edwin Church, ***Study for "The Icebergs,"*** ca. 1859.
Oil on canvas, 7⅛ × 12 in.
Courtesy, Olana State Historic Site, New York State Office of Parks, Recreation and Historic Preservation, OL.1980.1939.
Photograph by David C. Huntington.
Photograph courtesy of Gerald L. Carr.

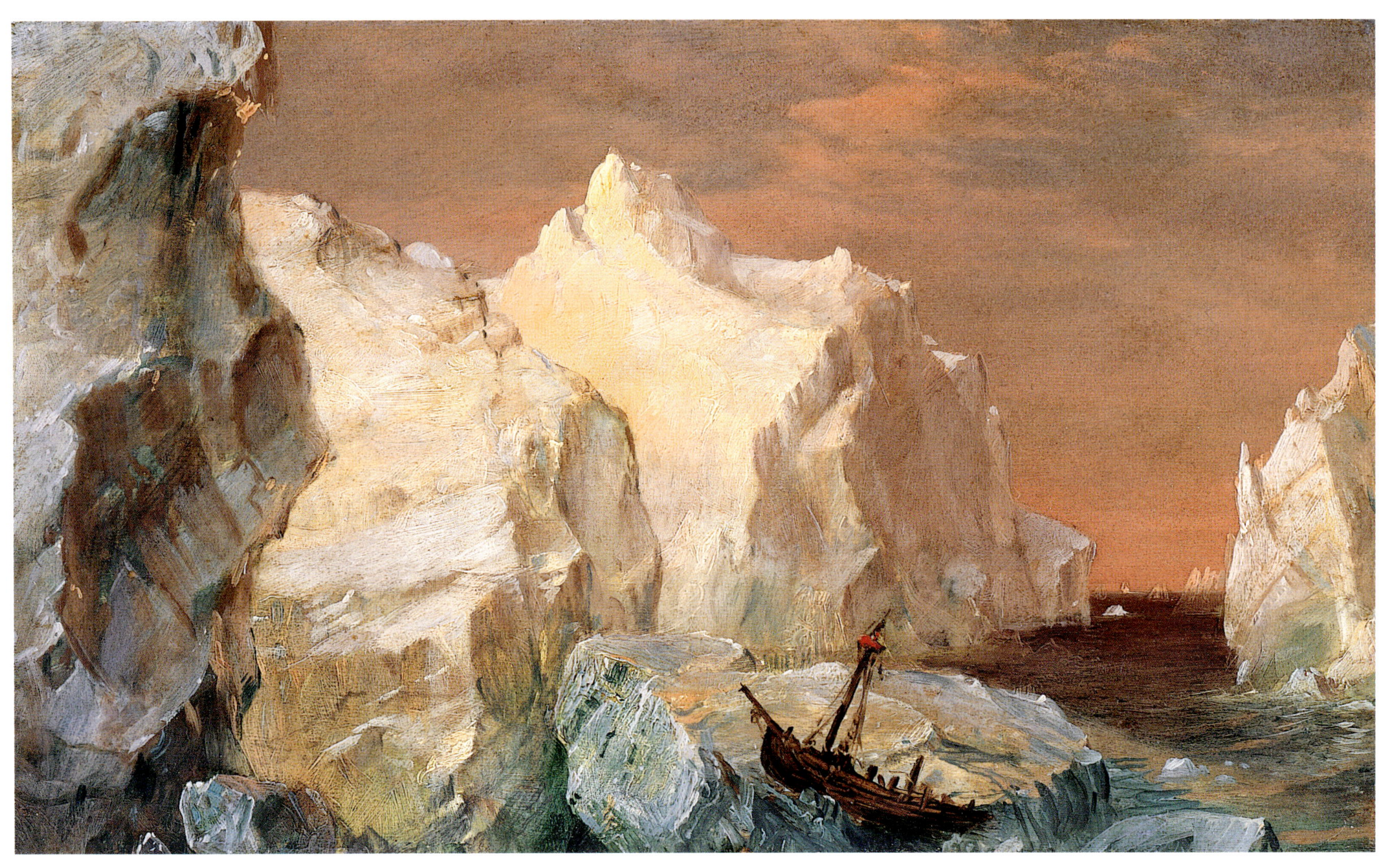

FIG. 28
Frederic Edwin Church, ***Icebergs and Wreck in Sunset,*** 1860.
Oil on paperboard mounted on canvas, 8⅛ × 13 in.
Courtesy of the Thyssen-Bornemisza Collection, Lugano, Switzerland.

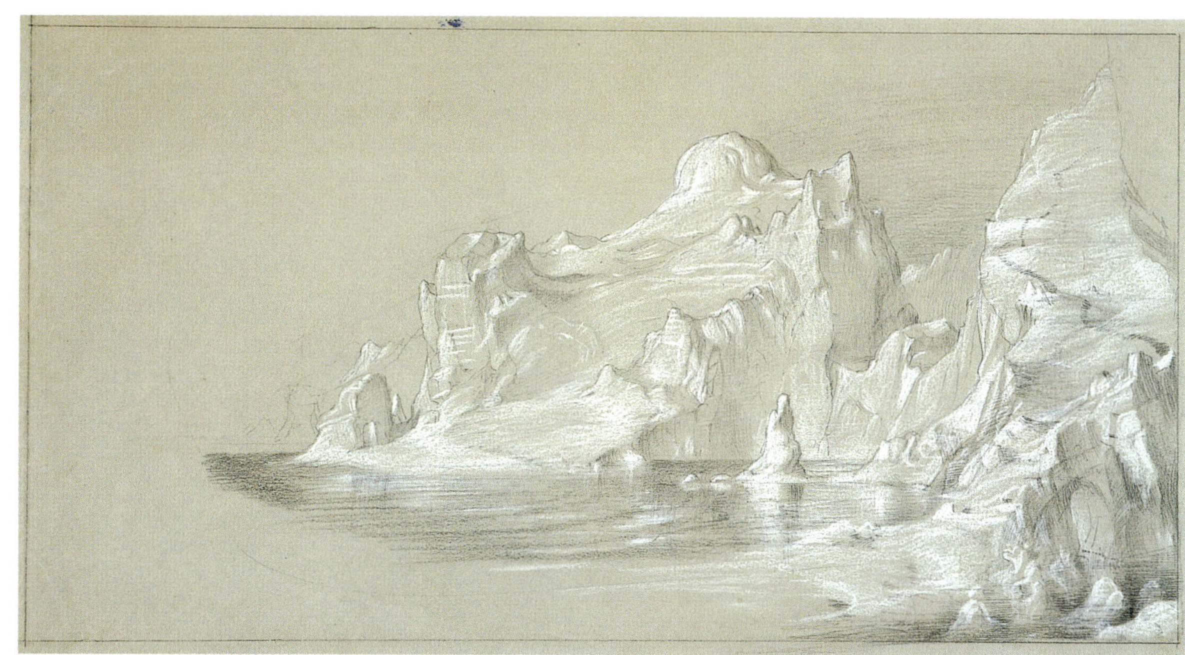

FIG. 29
Frederic Edwin Church, ***Study for "The Icebergs,"*** 1860.
Graphite and gouache on paper, 12⅝ × 19⅜ in.
Courtesy, Olana State Historic Site, New York State Office of Parks, Recreation and Historic Preservation, OL.1977.145.

the deliberate decision to exclude any direct reference to the legion of Arctic explorers who had attempted to find a navigable Northwest Passage.

Church finally settled on the configuration of the central dome of the iceberg in a pair of sketches, one in pencil, the other in oil (figs. 29, 30). In these sketches Church's ideas crystallized, and together they form the genesis of *The Icebergs*.

Although few people caught a glimpse of the work in progress, speculation about the painting abounded in the art press. An anonymous article called "The Iceberg of Torbay," published in the *Atlantic Monthly* in October 1860, included thinly veiled references to the artist "C—" that fooled no one, which was the point entirely. Church's whereabouts were carefully recounted in the New York press, and notices such as this, anticipating the completion of *The Icebergs*, removed any lingering ambiguity.[8] Noble's book-length narrative, *After Icebergs with a Painter* (fig. 31), appeared just weeks before the debut of Church's new painting. Illustrated with lithographs after Church's Arctic drawings (fig. 32), Noble's book, which recorded Church's "season among the icebergs, in which he was again discoverer, pioneer, conqueror,"[9] assured that the debut of *The Icebergs* was an event eagerly anticipated by the New York art world.

Church needed all his marketing skills for his Arctic masterpiece, for twelve days before its debut the bombardment of Fort Sumter realigned the nation's priorities. The shock of a nation finding itself at war rippled through the art market. Church went ahead with the unveiling of his painting at

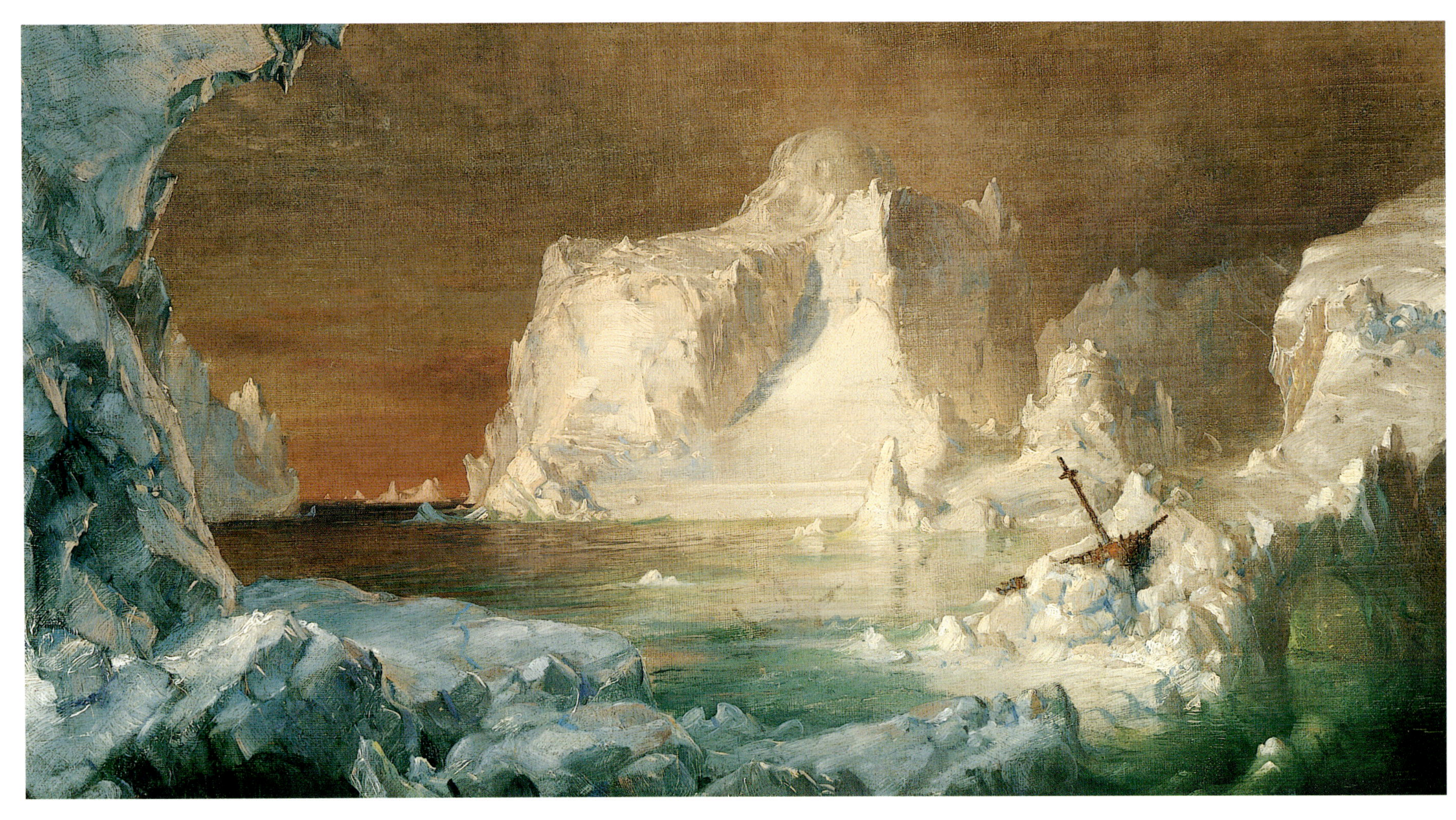

FIG. 30
Frederic Edwin Church, ***Study for "The Icebergs,"*** 1860.
Oil on canvas, 10 × 18¼ in.
Private collection.

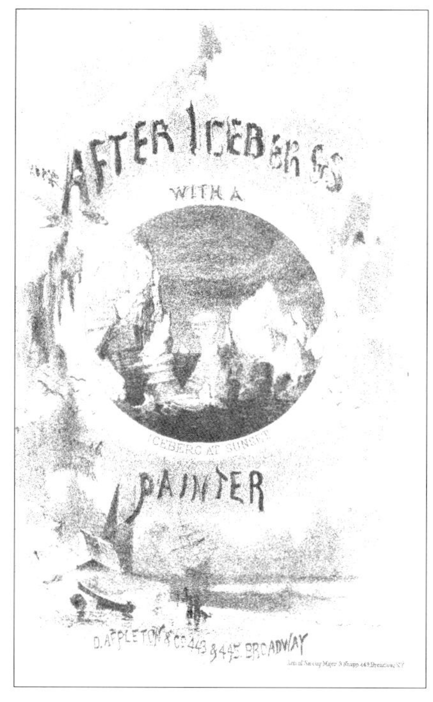

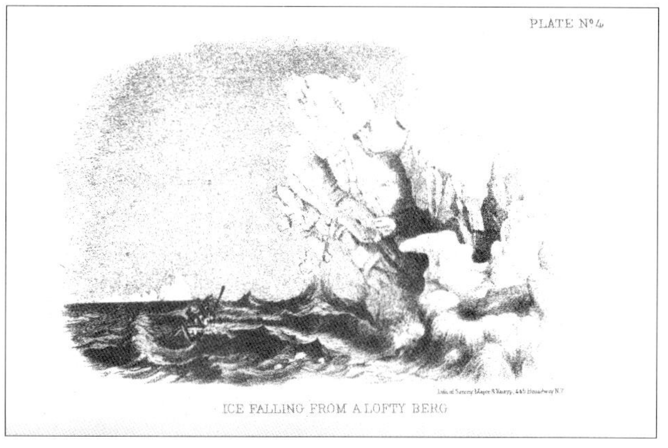

FINE ARTS.

WILL CLOSE WEDNESDAY, MAY 1,

"THE HEART OF THE ANDES,"

AT LOW'S BUILDING,

Corner of Court and Joralemon streets, Brooklyn.

"THE NORTH."

CHURCH'S PICTURE OF

ICEBERGS.

Exhibited for the benefit of the PATRIOTIC FUND, at GOUPIL'S, 772 Broadway.

J. McCLURE, Publisher.

Goupil's Gallery in New York as scheduled on April 24.[10] However, he made a critical concession to current events, titling his painting *"The North." Church's Picture of Icebergs* (fig. 33).[11] An ardent Unionist, he went a step further, pledging to donate the proceeds from the exhibition to the newly created Union Patriotic Fund, which supported the families of Union soldiers. Curiously, the critics applauded this gesture, but few commented on the significance of the title. What they agreed on was the powerful impact of Church's painting, lauded as a masterful rendering of this frozen world. That impact was enhanced by Church's theatrical presentation, as one critic noted: "Entering the room we found the whole end of the apartment filled with a huge frame of dark wood—carved like a cabinet and draped with crimson. Through this carved wood-work, as through an open window, we looked at once, nearly two thousand miles away—to Labrador!"[12] The writer for the *New-York Daily Tribune* proclaimed it to be "the most splendid work of art that has as yet been produced in this country. . . . It is an absolutely wonderful picture, a work of genius that illustrates the time and the country producing it."[13]

Such a strategy was important to the critical success of the picture, as the subject struck some as difficult and unapproachable. Several observers noted the hurdles Church had to overcome in depicting a world made up almost entirely of water—frozen as ice, liquid in meltwater and the ocean, and vaporous in the cloudy sky.[14] Others noted that Church had made this unstable footing

FIG. 31
Frontispiece for Louis Legrand Noble, ***After Icebergs with a Painter*** (New York and London, 1861; reprint, New York: Olana Galleries, 1979).
Photograph courtesy of the Dallas Museum of Art.

FIG. 32
After Frederic Edwin Church, ***Ice Falling from a Lofty Berg***, 1861.
Lithograph from Louis Legrand Noble, *After Icebergs with a Painter* (New York and London, 1861; reprint, New York: Olana Galleries, 1979).
Photograph courtesy of the Dallas Museum of Art.

FIG. 33
Advertisement for the 1861 New York City debut of ***The Heart of the Andes*** and ***The Icebergs***, *New York Morning Express*, April 29, 1861.
Photograph courtesy of Gerald L. Carr.

THE NORTH.

Painted by F. E. Church, from Studies of Icebergs made in the Northern Seas, in the Summer of 1859.

I. THE FORM OF THE ICEBERG.

The spectator is supposed to be standing on the ice, in a bay of the berg. The several masses are parts of one immense berg. Imagine an amphitheatre, upon the lower steps of which you stand, and see the icy foreground at your feet, and gaze upon the surrounding masses, all uniting in one beneath the surface of the sea. To the left is overhanging, precipitous ice; to the right is a part of the upper surface of the berg. To that succeeds an inner gorge, running up between Alpine peaks. In front is the main portion of the berg, exhibiting ice-architecture in its vaster proportions. Thus the beholder has around him the manifold forms of the huge Greenland glacier after it has been launched upon the deep, and subjected, for a time, to the action of the elements — waves and currents, sunshine and storm.

II. MOTION OF THE ICEBERG.

Every falling mass disturbs the exact balance of the berg upon its centre, far down in the sea. Large portions are supposed to have fallen, recently, from the side on which the spectator stands, giving preponderance to the opposite side. That has gone down; this has risen. All the foreground has risen out of the waves — the arch with its bridge and bowlder, and the lower part of the great central mass, as appears from the elevation and slant of the older water-lines.

III. SURFACE OF THE ICEBERG.

A berg does not break from its own weight, but explodes from the absorption of heat, and thaws and wears away. This affords every variety of surface. On the cliffs, to the left, is a fracture, fresh and sharp, cutting like newly-broken porcelain or glass. On the right are surfaces rounded and polished by the weather. In the foreground and arch are seen the effects of the surf and currents. Upon the central mass, in front, all varieties of surface are exhibited.

IV. COLORS OF THE ICEBERG.

With the exception of an occasional vein, which is blue as sapphire, or stains from rock, an iceberg is purely white, an opaque, dead white,— ghastly and spiritless in a dull atmosphere; but in bright weather, especially late in the afternoon, kindling with a varied splendor. The picture aims to represent the berg at that brilliant hour. Lights and shadows, hues and tints, shower the scene, and are thrown in all ways, and multiplied by reflection. The pale-blue bands, on the left, are the veins alluded to,— simply clear, transparent ice, formed in the cracks of the glacier. All the darker blues are only white ice under shadows. The green ice, as in the arch, is only green by reflection of the green water.

V. THE SEA.

From the brightness of an iceberg the eye is so affected that the sea appears very dark. Accordingly the beholder here looks out through a gradually widening avenue to the broad water, and finds it a very dark purple or violet. The sea, close in, partakes, with the surrounding ice, of all the brilliant reflections. Where the sea comes in contact with ice it is a lively green. Hence the emerald water of the foreground, and at the base of the great central mass. The pale-blue water just below the spectator, on the foreground, is an example of the pools of fresh water on the top of icebergs.

VI. THE SKY.

From the same optical causes that the sea is dark, the sky is sombre, rather than of a luminous azure. Fog, a feature of icebergs, is sweeping the heights in front, and reddening in the late afternoon light.

VII. EXPRESSION OF THE SCENE.

All things favoring, an iceberg, in itself alone, is a miracle of beauty and grandeur. A fine, quiet afternoon at sea affords all the requisites. Hence the picture presents the beholder with ice only, reposing, under the brightness of the declining sun, in the calm, solitary ocean,— grandeur with repose. The flight of the mist is noiseless. The swells come gently rolling in, in glassy circles, breaking with low murmur on the icy foreground.

On Exhibition at the BOSTON ATHENÆUM, Beacon Street.

Prentiss & Deland, Printers, 40, Congress Street.

FIG. 34

The North. *Painted by F. E. Church, from Studies of Icebergs made in the Northern Seas, in the Summer of 1859,* 1862.

Broadside announcement of the 1862 exhibition of ***The Icebergs*** at the Boston Athenæum (Boston: Prentiss & Deland Press, 1862).

Courtesy, Olana State Historic Site, New York State Office of Parks, Recreation and Historic Preservation, OL.1986.146.

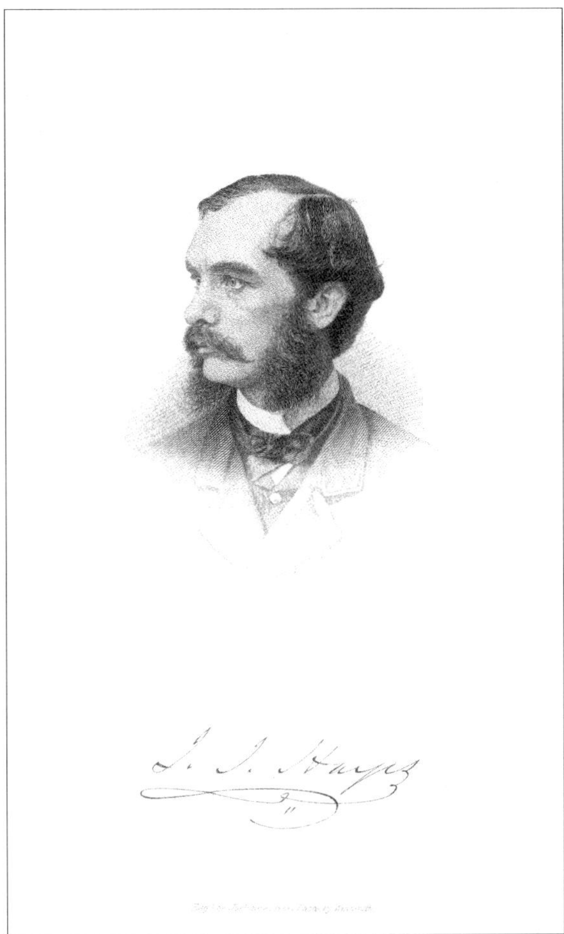

FIG. 35

Dr. Isaac Hayes

Engraving, frontispiece from Hayes, *The Open Polar Sea* (New York: Hurd & Houghton, 1867).

Photograph courtesy of the Dallas Museum of Art.

appear solidly grounded, creating the sense of a secure, if frozen, landscape of floating fragments of pack ice. Church did offer guidance to his audience by distributing a broadside, likely written by himself and Noble, that walks the viewer step by step into the painting's foreground, describing the mass, motion, colors, and dazzling optical effects of the berg (fig. 34).

Missing was any sign of human presence in the scene. At this point Church had not yet painted the broken mast now poignantly placed in the center foreground of the painting. Indeed, one reviewer observed "no trace whatever of human association, not a living creature of any description, no ship, no boat, not even the semblance of a wreck, no connecting link of any sort between them and the canvas. One brown boulder of rock, lodged on the ice, alone hints that the great, floating glacier was once in contact with earth."[15] The glacial erratic perched atop the ice cave on the right was the only bit of earth matter evident, viewed by some as a nod toward Church's interest in the emerging science of geology.

Church was a member of the American Geographical and Statistical Society, a group of scientists, artists, and literary men united in their fascination with the natural world. Church's long-standing interest in exploration, engendered by the writings of Alexander von Humboldt and his own forays into South America and Canada, made him a desirable colleague in such societies. Church counted among his friends the polar explorer Dr. Isaac Hayes (1832–1881), who commanded his own Arctic expedition in 1860 (fig. 35).[16] Hayes returned from this trip in October 1861, unaware that his country was at war with itself. Shortly thereafter he delivered a series of stirring lectures, concluding, "God willing, I trust yet to carry the flag of our great Republic, with not a single star erased from its glorious Union, to the extreme Northern limits of the earth."[17] Through Church's painting and Hayes's lectures, for many Americans the Arctic North and the Union North were inextricably intertwined.[18]

Hayes brought along another polar explorer to his lectures: his lead sled-dog, Oosisoak (fig. 36), depicted in a finished oil sketch Church completed in about two hours.[19] This engaging painting mimics the format and palette of so many of the portraits made of British Arctic explorers, shown frontally, dressed in their furs, against an icy backdrop.[20] Further, Hayes returned from his trip with sketches (figs. 37, 38) he supplied to Church for use in his next grand-scale Arctic painting, the *Aurora Borealis* of 1865 (fig. 39). Church's nocturnal scene, lit by the shimmering auroras, presents Hayes's ship, the *United States*, wintering over in the pack ice as the explorer's sled-dog team mushes toward home base. The distinctive pyramidal peak towering over the central cliffs is one Hayes named "Church's Peak" in honor of his friend.[21]

Despite the overall positive attention to the picture, *The North* did not find a buyer following either its New York debut or a subsequent showing in Boston between February and May 1862. Economic jitters and Church's presumed high price of about $10,000 evidently dampened enthusiasm for such a purchase, and the artist's plans to have a chromolithograph made for sale by subscription

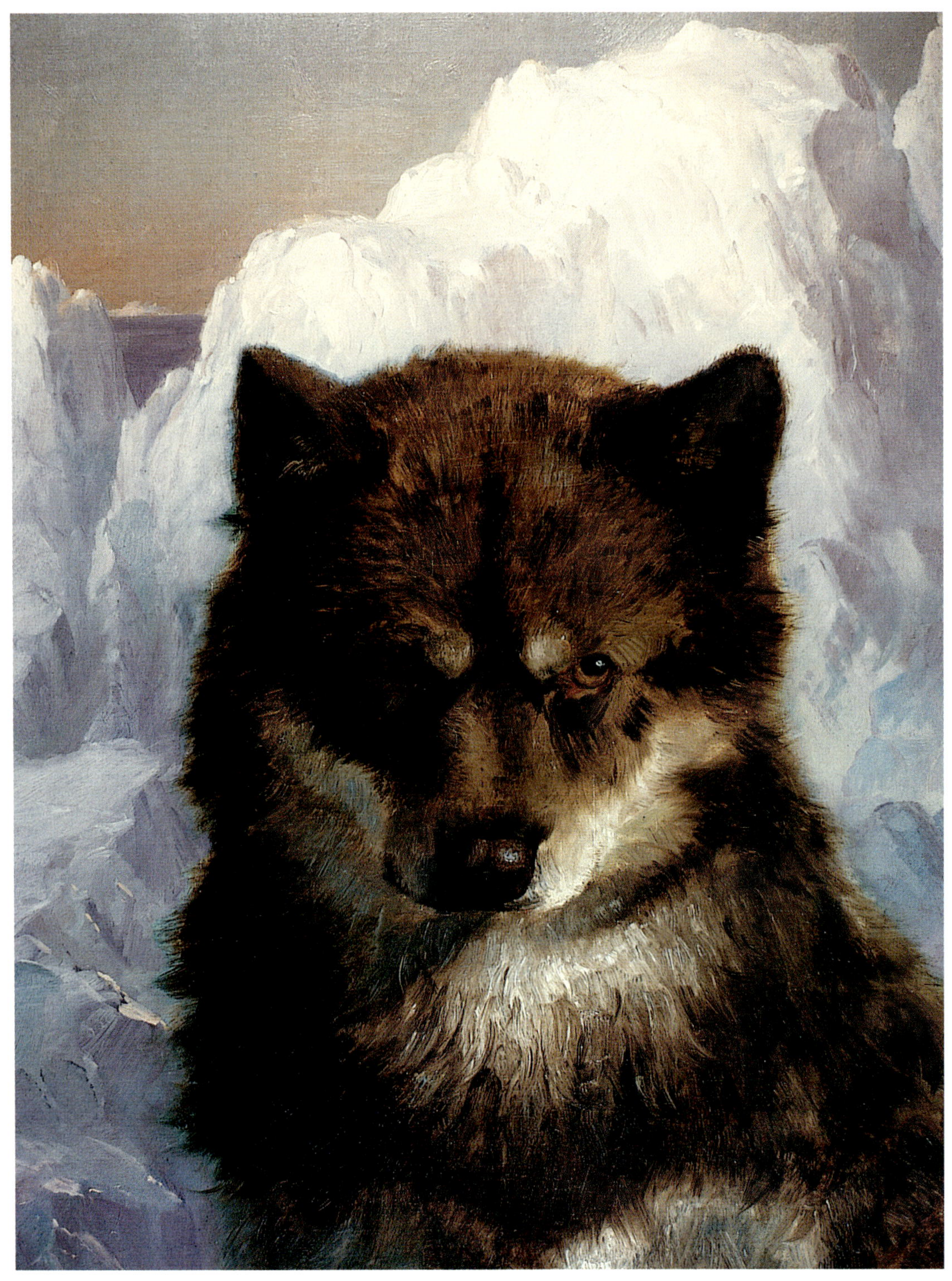

FIG. 36
Frederic Edwin Church, ***Oosisoak,***
ca. November 1861.
Oil on canvas, 23 × 17 in.
Private collection.
Photograph by David C. Huntington.
Photograph courtesy of Gerald L. Carr.

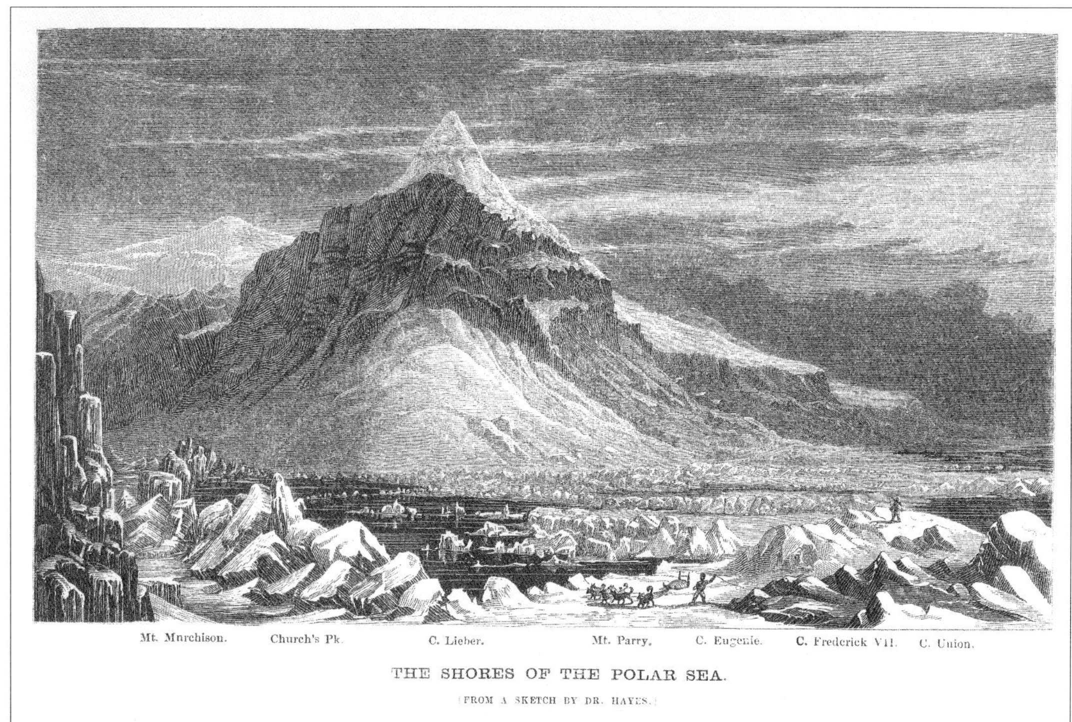

FIG. 37
After a sketch by Dr. Isaac Hayes, ***Church's Peak***, 1867.
Engraving from Hayes, *The Open Polar Sea* (New York: Hurd & Houghton, 1867).
Photograph courtesy of the Dallas Museum of Art.

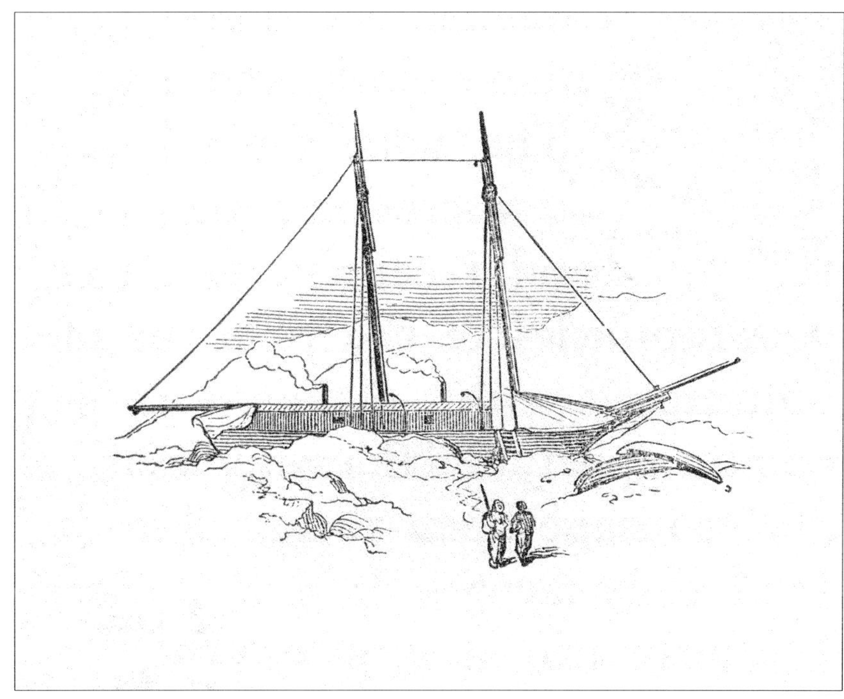

FIG. 38
After a sketch by Dr. Isaac Hayes, ***The Schooner "United States,"*** 1867.
Engraving from Hayes, *The Open Polar Sea* (New York: Hurd & Houghton, 1867).
Photograph courtesy of the Dallas Museum of Art.

were likewise shelved. Church found himself harboring his massive canvas for more than a year. Although it is not certain that the work took up space in his studio the entire time, it was clear to the artist that he needed to move the painting out to make space for others. Church's American patrons may not have felt comfortable spending so much money on a painting during the Civil War, but the artist knew he had a strong following in England. Beginning with *Niagara* in 1857 and *The Heart of the Andes* in 1859, Church had sent each of his "Great Pictures" to London, where they were displayed as singular objects for admiration. In 1863 Church contracted with his agent, John McClure, to send *The North* to London as well.

In the course of those negotiations, Church made two crucial decisions. One was to retitle the painting, reverting to *The Icebergs*. Church recognized that England's foreign policy favored the Confederacy. By 1863 England was considering establishing a naval blockade off the coast of Virginia to protect its interest in raw cotton from the South destined for British textile mills. The other was to paint the broken mast of a ship in the center foreground, presumably to commemorate those intrepid Arctic explorers who had lost their lives attempting to find the fabled Northwest Passage across the Arctic archipelago.[22] In June 1863 the newly christened *Icebergs* opened at the German Gallery, on New Bond Street in London (fig. 4), to glowing reviews, but British press reports made no mention of either alteration.[23]

The London preview party for *The Icebergs* was attended by many of the surviving Arctic exploration luminaries, including Lady Franklin, Sir Leopold McClintock, Dr. John Rae, Sir George Back, Sir Edward Belcher, and Sir Richard Collinson, and the noted expert on glaciers Professor John Tyndall.[24] As had been the case with his other "Great Pictures," Church's painting of icebergs was well received. Church revived his agent's plans to have the work reproduced as a chromolithograph, at the time the most advanced form of color reproduction available (fig. 40). The London lithography firm of Charles Day & Son displayed the painting after the exhibition closed, while it worked on the chromolithograph. In January 1865 the news appeared in Boston that the print was newly available for purchase but that few copies were left.[25] At some point during this period, Sir Edward William Watkin (1819–1901), a Member of Parliament, purchased *The Icebergs* and shipped it to Rose Hill, his country estate outside Manchester.

Watkin (fig. 10) was neither a prominent art collector nor involved with Arctic exploration. However, he was no stranger to the United States and Canada. In 1861 he was a director and manager of the Grand Trunk Railway of Canada, a precursor of the present-day Canadian Pacific.[26] He also played a crucial, yet understated, role in the creation of the dominion of Canada between 1861 and 1867, for which he received a knighthood in 1868, and he was made a baronet in 1880.[27] The year after he purchased *The Icebergs*, Watkin traveled to the United States with a group of British entrepreneurs interested in evaluating the feasibility of investing in an ambitious expansion of the American railroads. On the night of October 30, 1865, this group hosted a farewell dinner held at Delmonico's that boasted

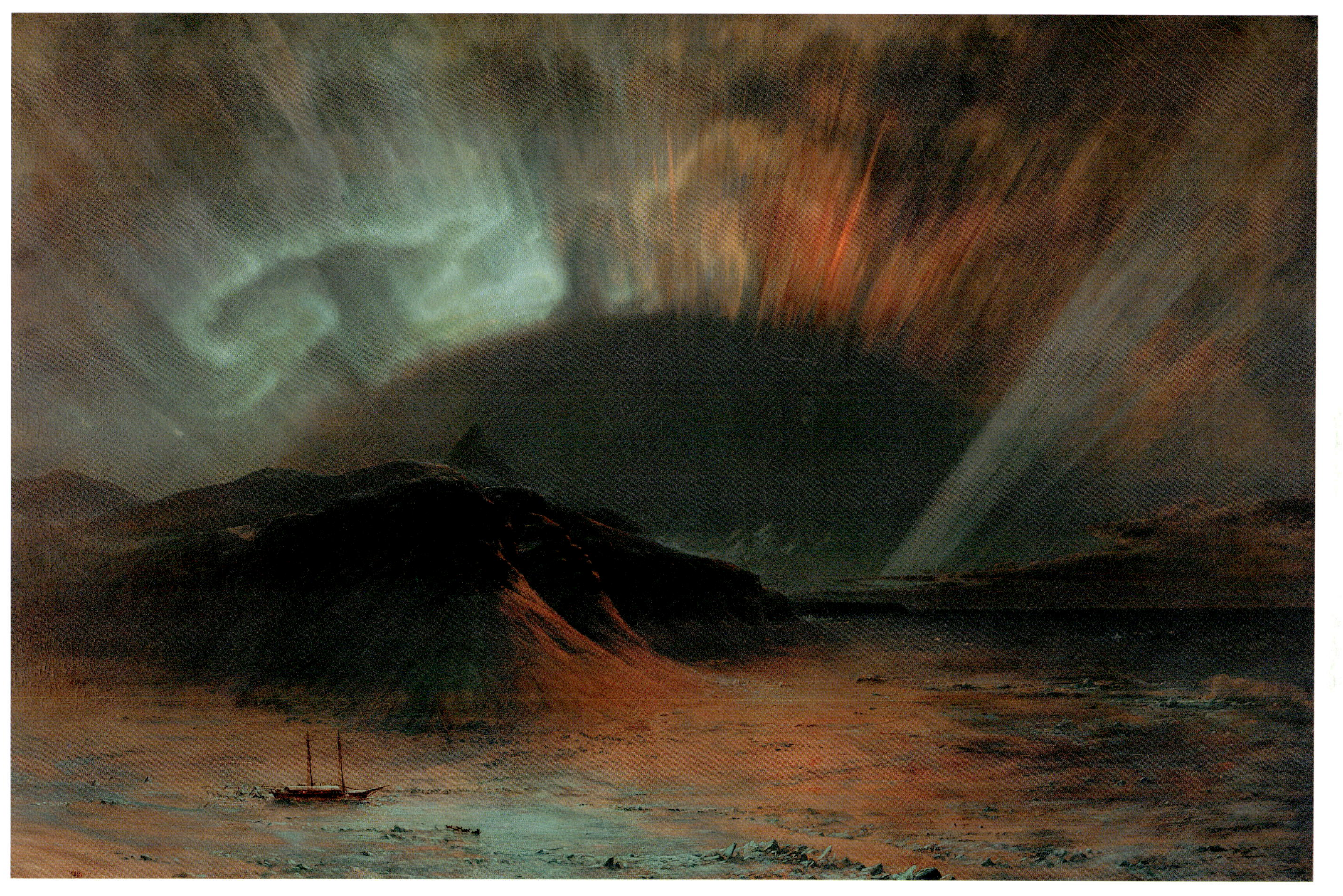

FIG. 39
Frederic Edwin Church, ***Aurora Borealis,*** 1865.
Oil on canvas, 56⅛ × 83⅜ in.
Smithsonian American Art Museum, Gift of Eleanor Blodgett.

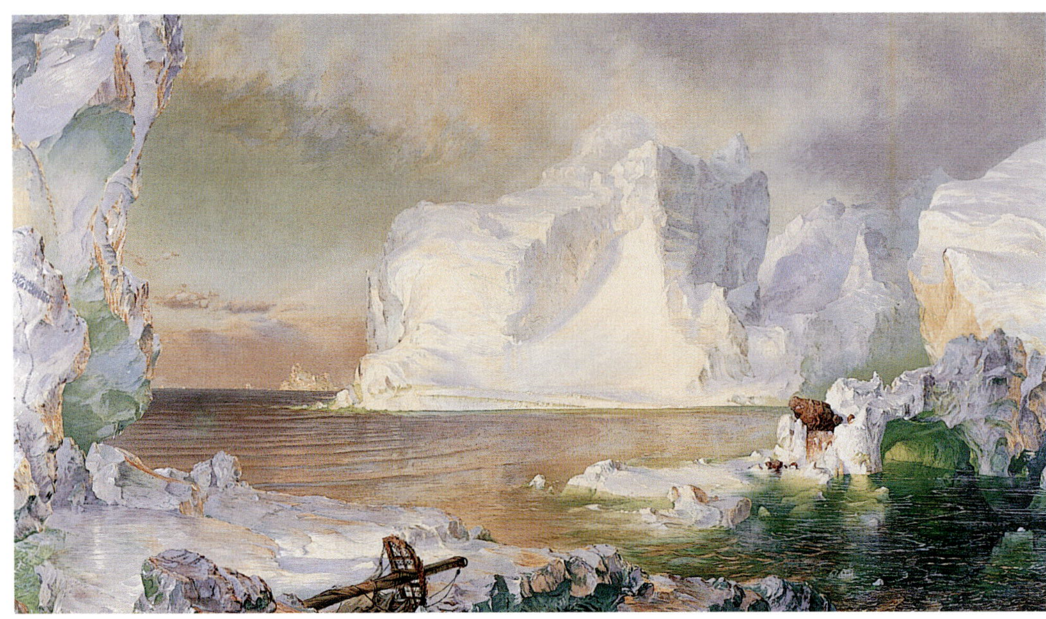

FIG. 40
Charles Risdon, after Frederic Edwin Church, ***The Icebergs (The North)***, 1864.
Chromolithograph, 21 × 35½ in.
Private collection.
Photograph courtesy of the Dallas Museum of Art.

a guest list of 250 luminaries including ex-president Millard Fillmore, Generals Grant and Sherman, the literary giant William Cullen Bryant, and the artists Daniel Huntington, president of the NAD, and Albert Bierstadt.[28] Three years later, Watkin attended a lavish dinner in London hosted by Bierstadt to honor the American author Henry Wadsworth Longfellow, an event also attended by the politician William Gladstone, the poet Robert Browning, and the artist Sir Edwin Landseer.[29] A London newspaper article in 1891 indicated that Watkin and his wife had long held soirées at Rose Hill, paying what is, for now, the only known compliment to "the fine canvases which dignify [the] picture gallery."[30]

Sir Edward acquired his cultural interests honestly. At twenty-one he became a director of the Manchester Athenæum and organized literary events in 1843–44 featuring the disparate talents of the author Charles Dickens, the politician Benjamin Disraeli, the philosopher Sir Archibald Alison, and the satirist George Cruikshank.[31] The following year he helped found the *Manchester Examiner* newspaper. Still, his accomplishments as a politician and railway magnate overshadow these early achievements. Watkin's political career began when he was seventeen and included several separate stints as a Member of Parliament beginning in the 1850s. In 1845 he also began a long and illustrious career in the British railway business, serving no fewer than seven British railway companies over the years. In 1863 Watkin rejoined the Manchester, Sheffield, and Lincolnshire Railway Company, retaining the position of chairman until 1894.[32] As a result, he was affectionately known as "the Railway King" and tried repeatedly (without success) to secure permission to begin work on a proposed channel tunnel linking Calais to Dover.[33]

Watkin's interest in *The Icebergs* may well have been inspired by his 1861 trip to Canada. His investments in the burgeoning railroad industry had prompted the trip, along with his confidential work on behalf of confederation. On that transatlantic crossing he had seen icebergs from the deck of the ship, and in his journal entry for August 11, 1861, he wrote,

> We had heard at Queenstown, from a note . . . that icebergs had been seen on the homeward passage, and at about 3 o'clock we saw ahead of us something that looked like the wreck of a steamer—but it was pronounced to be ice. It was about 10 miles off. . . . As soon as we got abreast of it, we saw pack ice around it, and the light, then shining upon the whole mass, gave a fairy-like whiteness,—transparent, snowy whiteness—which was very beautiful to see. While we were observing it, a great mass broke away, toppled over into the sea, sending up an immense snowy spray, and disappeared. The remainder stayed in sight, with the evening sun-light upon it, for a couple of hours.[34]

Watkin might as well have been describing *The Icebergs* itself.

Watkin's involvement with the railroads in Britain and North America and his privileged role in the confederation of Canada likely fueled his compulsion to own *The Icebergs*. His work with the Grand Trunk Railroad—now the Canadian Pacific—provides the key. Watkin noted in his published journal that with the development of the trans-Canada railway system, "The problem of a 'North-west Passage' has been solved in a new and better way. It is no longer a question of threading dark and dismal seas within the limits of Arctic ice and snow, doubtful to find, and impossible, if found, to navigate."[35] Considered in that light, *The Icebergs* symbolizes the heroic efforts expended to find the seaward passage and the magnitude of the achievement represented by its overland realization. For Church, *The Icebergs* served as an understated memorial to Sir John Franklin and those who assailed the Arctic in search of him; for Watkin, it positioned him as the natural inheritor of their quest.

Neither man rested on those laurels. Church's subsequent commissions, *Cotopaxi* (The Detroit Institute of Arts) in 1862, *Chimborazo* (The Huntington Library, Art Collections, and Botanical Gardens, San Marino, Calif.) in 1864, and *Aurora Borealis* (fig. 39) in 1865 reaffirmed the fundamental soundness of the artist's career and his marketability. This trio allowed Church to reach a crescendo in 1865, when he arranged to have all three exhibited as a group in London. The reviews were everything the artist could have wanted.[36] From that point, his career, like those of so many Hudson River School painters, began to wane. There were successes, to be sure, but by the 1880s he lived in virtual seclusion at his country home, Olana, all but forgotten by men of art. As for Watkin, his political career sustained him for more than forty years, but with his wife's death in 1888, his energy for public life diminished. When Watkin died in 1901, he and *The Icebergs* disappeared from view.

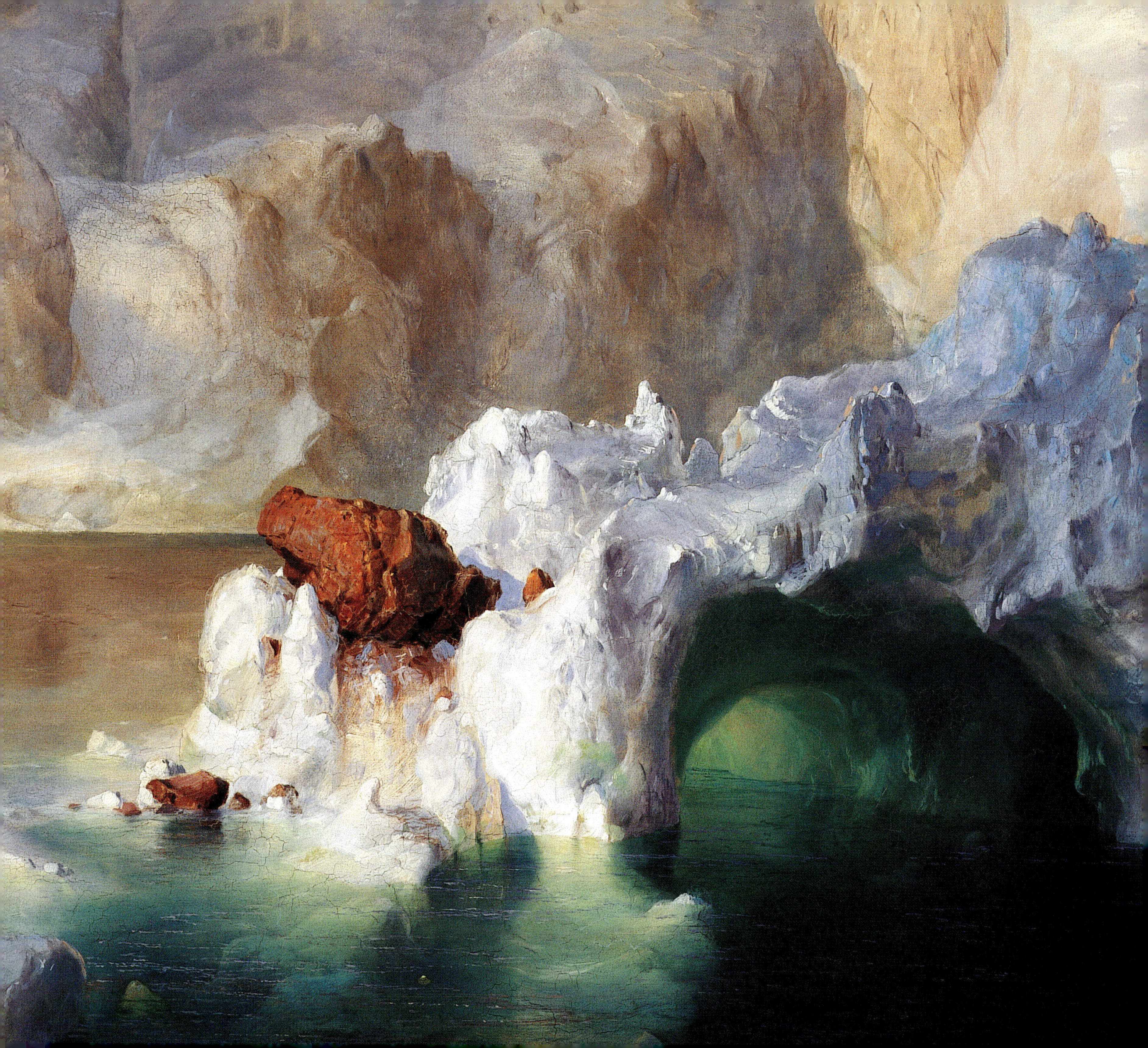

Eleanor Jones Harvey

THE OTHER *Seven-Eighths*

During the final quarter of the nineteenth century, the Hudson River School of painting fell out of favor, replaced by a new generation of popular artists and styles. Church lived to fulminate against impressionism, but his voice was lost in the excitement surrounding this new way of seeing the world. The Armory Show of 1913 introduced America to the intoxicating power of painterly abstraction in the work of Marcel Duchamp and Wassily Kandinsky, and by World War II America was arguing the merits of Jackson Pollock. Against this backdrop, there was little effort to reexamine mid-nineteenth-century painting until the 1950s, when a generation of young scholars began writing dissertations on previously celebrated American artists like Thomas Cole, Albert Bierstadt, and Frederic Church, then all but lost to history. Their work dovetailed with the interests of collectors who were also beginning to turn to these neglected artists and their relatively inexpensive paintings. By the 1970s, the market for American painting centered on the resurgence of mid-nineteenth-century landscape, genre, and still-life paintings.

It was only in 1960, when David C. Huntington completed his landmark dissertation on Frederic Church, that Church and, by extension, the midcentury genre of landscape painting would once again move to the forefront of the study of American art. Six years later, Huntington followed his dissertation with the first monograph and exhibition of Church's works since the artist's death. He put the chromolithograph of the missing *Icebergs* on the dust jacket of his book, hoping that someone would recognize the painting and contact him with news of its whereabouts. His hopes were

(DETAIL)
Frederic Edwin Church,
The Icebergs, 1861.
Oil on canvas, 64½ × 112½ in.
Dallas Museum of Art, Anonymous gift, 1979.28.

well founded; during that decade numerous important paintings by Church and others emerged from family collections that had long been shrouded in privacy.

The story of Church's *Twilight in the Wilderness* (fig. 26) is perhaps the best example. Richard Weimann, a dealer from Connecticut with a background in intelligence work, found it and an impressive number of "lost" paintings by Church. Working from nineteenth-century records, he unearthed several paintings, including *Rainy Season in the Tropics* (Fine Arts Museums of San Francisco) and *Jerusalem* (The Nelson-Atkins Museum of Art, Kansas City), by tracing them through the families of the original owners, often working closely with members of Church's extended family. In 1965 he found *Twilight in the Wilderness* in a hunting lodge in Maine that belonged to descendants of the first owner. He carefully packed his prize, tied it to the roof rack on his car, and drove it to Manhattan. Although initially he had difficulty selling the picture, its acquisition by the Cleveland Museum of Art helped resuscitate interest in Church's paintings.[37]

The strengthening market for major American paintings, spurred by the bicentennial in 1976 and the growth of American art departments in auction houses, was one motivating factor for such searches. As a groundswell of interest in mid-nineteenth-century American art developed, museums and collectors yearned for, and paid record prices for, landscapes, still lifes, and genre scenes. The other motivation, not unlike the pull of the Arctic region, was the desire to find what appeared to be lost forever, the thrill of sailing uncharted waters, following thin leads, and using information and determination to achieve one's ends.

In this regard, *The Icebergs* was one of a long line of such lost masterpieces, and who better than Richard Weimann to embark on the quest? The key to his earlier successes had been to track a painting's whereabouts by following the family tree of its original owner or tracing the ownership of a family home. Weimann adopted the same approach with *The Icebergs*. It was common knowledge among Church enthusiasts that the trail had gone cold with confusion over the identity of the original purchaser of the painting. In 1867 the influential historian Henry Tuckerman had published the owner's name as "Mr. Watson, M.P., of London";[38] the *Boston Sunday Herald* attempted to correct this when it referred to him in 1890 as "Sir Edward Watkins, M.P. of London."[39] Weimann researched every "Watson" he could plausibly match to the painting's whereabouts, including the shipper who took the painting from New York to London.[40] At some point he also researched Sir Edward William Watkin, going so far as to drive to Manchester and ask for help in finding his house. Misdirected to an adjacent building, he gave up his search as yet another blind alley.[41]

As Weimann was conducting his sleuthing, Sandra Feldman had begun her own search, operating with a similar rationale. Feldman was a talented researcher at Hirschl & Adler Galleries in New York. In 1977, with the art dealer Jay Maroney's encouragement, she asked gallery partner Stuart Feld if she might try to find *The Icebergs*.[42] Feld agreed to underwrite her research.[43] Feldman began by casting a broad net. She compiled references published in England and the United States reporting on the whereabouts of *The Icebergs* after its London debut. Simultaneously, she focused on the three Parliamentarians in the 1860s whose surnames begin with "W": Watkin, Watkins, and Watson. Noting that in nineteenth-century script, the lowercase letters "s" and "k" could easily be confused, she realized Tuckerman could have misread those letters and transcribed "Watkin" as "Watson." She established biographies of all three men and went to Somerset House in London to read each man's will, in an effort to determine who might fit the profile of the owner of such a painting by assessing his net worth and possessions.

From her earlier research on Albert Bierstadt's monumental *Mt. Rosalie* (Brooklyn Museum of Art), Feldman knew that several of Britain's leading railroad magnates had been active collectors of American paintings. When she discovered that Sir Edward William Watkin was a railroad investor and a Member of Parliament, she felt she had found her man. Her study of his finances made it clear that he possessed the means and the cultural background for such a purchase.[44] In the British Library she found an elusive copy of Watkin's travel memoirs. There she found the passage quoted in this book on page 69, describing his encounter with icebergs on his transatlantic crossing in 1861.[45] Convinced she was on the right track, she began to contact every known address for Watkin—in London, Folkestone (where he kept a resort home), and Manchester—and research his descendants, hoping one of them might still own *The Icebergs*.[46]

Since Watkin had maintained a country residence in Manchester and served as Member of Parliament for the region, she requested help from the city of Manchester. Through the city librarian she learned that Watkin's estate, Rose Hill, had become a remand center, a detention facility for boys. In the years since Watkin's death, the structure had served as a home for unwed mothers, an ophthalmic hospital, a convalescent home, an orphanage, and finally a residential assessment center for delinquent boys.[47] She and Stuart Feld were convinced that the painting's presumed size and the attendant difficulty of moving it might mean the painting had been left in one of Watkin's houses and conveyed with the property.[48] She made inquiries about gaining access to the facility but was discouraged from doing so by D. Taylor, the local history librarian in Manchester, and never made her petition in person.[49] Instead, from London she called Rose Hill and spoke with Mair Baulch, the matron, who in 1977 had no particular reason to know whether the painting was under her roof. No, she said, there was no such painting as *The Icebergs* at Rose Hill.[50]

Almost a year later, in a letter to Taylor of May 31, 1978, Feldman made her case for suspecting that *The Icebergs* was either at Rose Hill, the local parish church, or somewhere else in the suburb of Northenden. If she returned to England in August, would the librarian accompany her and help her get into Rose Hill?[51] Taylor's reply was a blow to her hopes. Writing of his doubts that pursuing Watkin would bear fruit, he dissuaded her from following up the Rose Hill lead, adding that he did not have the time to accompany her on a site visit.[52] Despite not going to Manchester, Feldman continued her research.

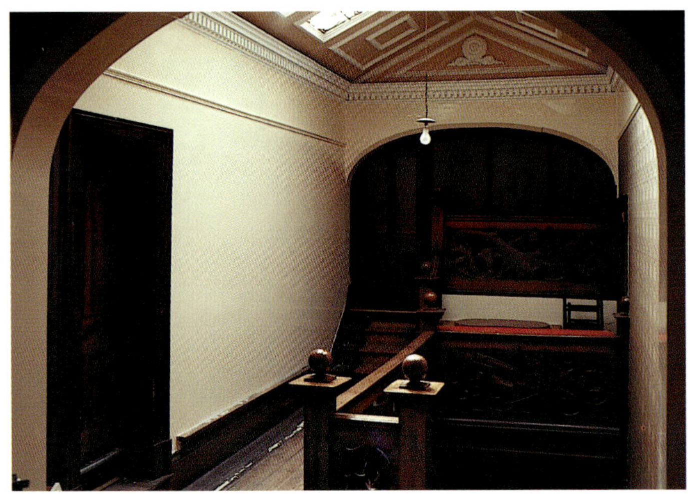

FIG. 41
Rose Hill, Northenden, near Manchester, main staircase showing the wall (left) on which ***The Icebergs*** hung, 1980.
Photograph courtesy of Gerald L. Carr.

By that fall, however, Mrs. Baulch did have reason to focus on a large, dingy painting hanging on a little-used upper staircase. She had found a run-down stone cottage in the Lake District that she wanted to purchase for Rose Hill. Most of the boys in her care were from the inner city; the Lake District property would be an opportunity for them to renovate it and spend some time in the country. Her goal was a modest one: to raise roughly £14,000. Noting the inscription on the ice in the foreground, *F. E. Church, 1861,* she conducted some research on the painting and discovered that Church was an American artist. Some five years earlier she had visited the Art Institute of Chicago and had been enthralled by the museum's collection of impressionist paintings. Remembering that experience, in early November 1978 she wrote a letter to the museum, enclosing a photograph of *The Icebergs*, and inquired if there was any interest in it. Over the next few months, she and the curator of American art, Milo Naeve, corresponded, discussing the painting's history and its condition. The conversation gradually moved toward negotiation of a price for the painting. In May 1979 Naeve and Marshall Field, a member of the Art Institute's board of trustees, flew to Manchester for a firsthand look. By this time the Manchester City Council had gotten involved with the fate of the painting, and the Art Institute's first offer was refused. Ron Hall, the assistant director in the city's Social Services Department, suggested contacting British art experts to evaluate the painting. Although the Art Institute persisted in its efforts to buy the painting, Hall decided to call Sotheby's, an auction house in London.[53]

Thus it happened that in early June 1979 James Miller, a paintings specialist at Sotheby's who handled American paintings that came to light in Great Britain, was asked to look at a painting in Manchester. It was described to him as a ship down in the water, signed by "Church." He then received a photograph of the painting. He dimly recalled the chromolithograph that had appeared on

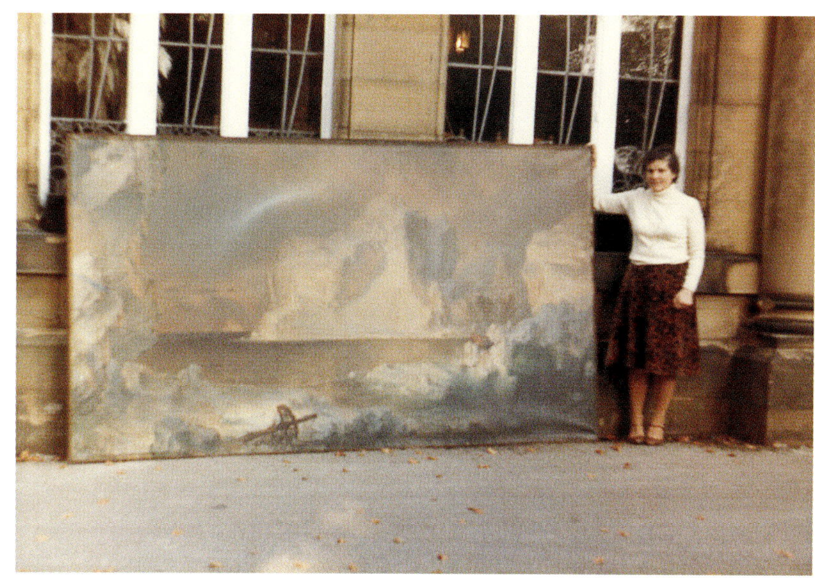

FIG. 42
Mair Baulch standing next to ***The Icebergs*** outside Rose Hill, Northenden, Manchester, 1978.
Photograph courtesy of Glen Baulch.

the cover of Huntington's 1966 book on Church, and that the painting was last seen in England. The caller indicated that an offer for the painting had been made. Would Miller come take a look?

Miller, who was new to the job and keen to establish his credentials, took the train to Manchester the next day. When he arrived at Rose Hill, he found the painting hanging, unframed, on a dark staircase (fig. 41). Even though the painting did not show to its best advantage, he realized it was a significant picture. He asked to have it taken outdoors and there explained to the Baulches that this was in fact a long-lost painting by the American artist Frederic Church (fig. 42). He felt confident estimating on the spot that the painting had a value of at least $500,000 and suggested the Baulches put it in the city art museum for safekeeping. He also examined the painting, which he determined to be in remarkably good condition, and realized that a light cleaning would reveal a spectacular picture.[54]

The director of the Manchester City Art Gallery at the time was Timothy Clifford, who is now director-general of the National Galleries of Scotland. Clifford and Miller knew each other from their school days, and *The Icebergs* moved swiftly from the front lawn of Rose Hill to the secure environs of the museum.[55] Clifford, who had no prior knowledge of the painting, agreed that it was a major work. He installed *The Icebergs* in his spacious offices. There in a grand room with a painted coffered ceiling, *The Icebergs* held court. Meanwhile, Clifford was making his own pitch to keep the painting, which had already been identified as city property by the Manchester City Council. Clifford argued that such a valuable work should remain on display for the public benefit as part of the museum's permanent collection. However, the estimated value and the proposals that had already surfaced about how to use the expected windfall from its sale doomed his entreaties.[56]

When Miller returned to London, he verified his hunch about the identity of the painting. Realizing the picture would most likely fetch a higher price in New York than in London, he began the process to obtain an export license. In the morning's interoffice mail, he sent a photograph of the painting to his counterparts in New York, along with the memorably dry comment, "Presumably this should come to you for sale."[57] Grete Meilman and Peter Rathbone, who together ran the American paintings department at Sotheby's in New York, could not believe their good fortune—the painting had quite literally landed in their laps. Meilman stayed up until 3 A.M. to call Miller in London as soon as he got to work the next morning and, after hearing his story, booked a flight to Manchester, taking a signed contract with her.[58] In late June the Manchester City Council agreed to send the painting to New York to be auctioned.

It did not take long before the news surfaced that *The Icebergs* had been found. The Manchester newspapers broke the story in articles dated July 6 and 7, 1979.[59] Stuart Feld was telephoned with the news. He tried to persuade the Manchester City Council and Mrs. Baulch to let him handle the sale of the painting, but to no avail.[60] By early August *The Icebergs* had been shipped to Sotheby's in New York. Peter Rathbone called David Huntington, then a professor of art history at the University of Michigan, with the news. Huntington, who did not travel to New York frequently, sped to the city to see for himself.[61] Feldman, who had spent two years chasing *The Icebergs* and had pinpointed its whereabouts a calendar year earlier, had to settle for the satisfaction of having been right, rather than the euphoria of making the discovery. *The Icebergs* had been rediscovered, not ultimately through art historical sleuthing, but because Mair Baulch had brought it to the world's attention.

As Weimann had found with *Twilight in the Wilderness*, *The Icebergs* had stayed with the house. When Sir Edward William Watkin died at Rose Hill in April 1901, his son, Sir Alfred Mellor Watkin, inherited the property and its contents. The following year he sold the estate to William Joseph Parkyn, J.P. When Parkyn sold the property to the Manchester Guardians of the Poor in 1915, he offered *The Icebergs* as a gift "in Perpetuity" to St. Wilfred's Church in Northenden. Six years later the church returned the painting to Rose Hill, which was under the purview of the city of Manchester Social Services Committee.[62] There it had remained until 1979, a part of the building's fabric, lost in plain view.

The first American press coverage of the discovery appeared in mid-August, when the *New York Times* ran a short article, presumably scripted by Sotheby's, suggesting the painting might sell for a new record price.[63] The records set in American art were far lower than those for European paintings. The top price for one of Church's paintings up to that time was $230,000, for *New England Landscape* (fig. 43), painted about 1849.[64] By contrast, Albert Bierstadt weighed in with an auction record of $115,000, set in 1975.[65] In the genre of still life, the top price of $300,000 was for a work by William Michael Harnett, set in April 1979.[66] The previous year, Hirschl & Adler Galleries had paid $980,000

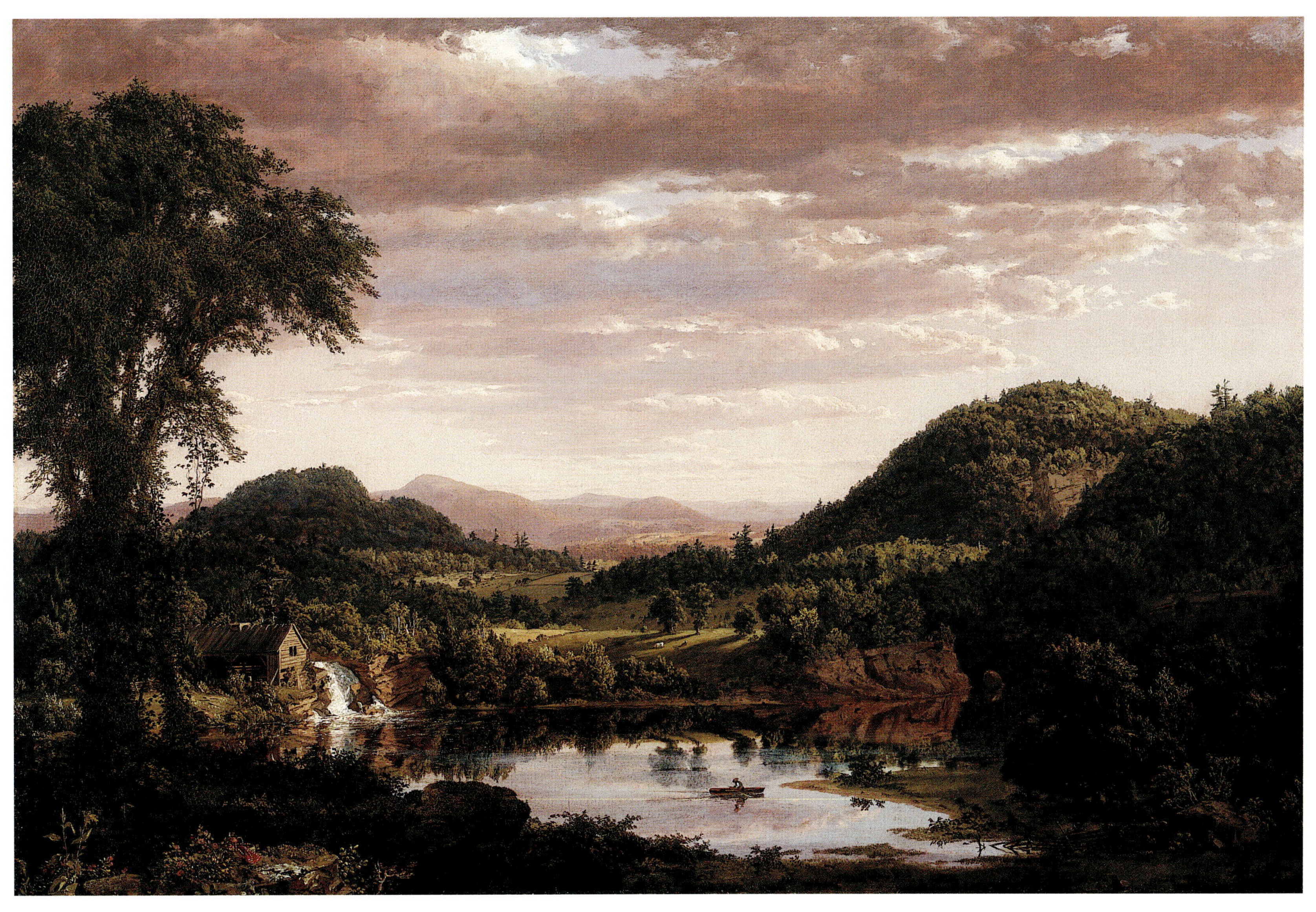

FIG. 43
Frederic Edwin Church, ***New England Landscape,*** ca. 1849.
Oil on canvas, 25⅛ × 36¼ in.
Amon Carter Museum, Fort Worth, Texas, 1979.11.

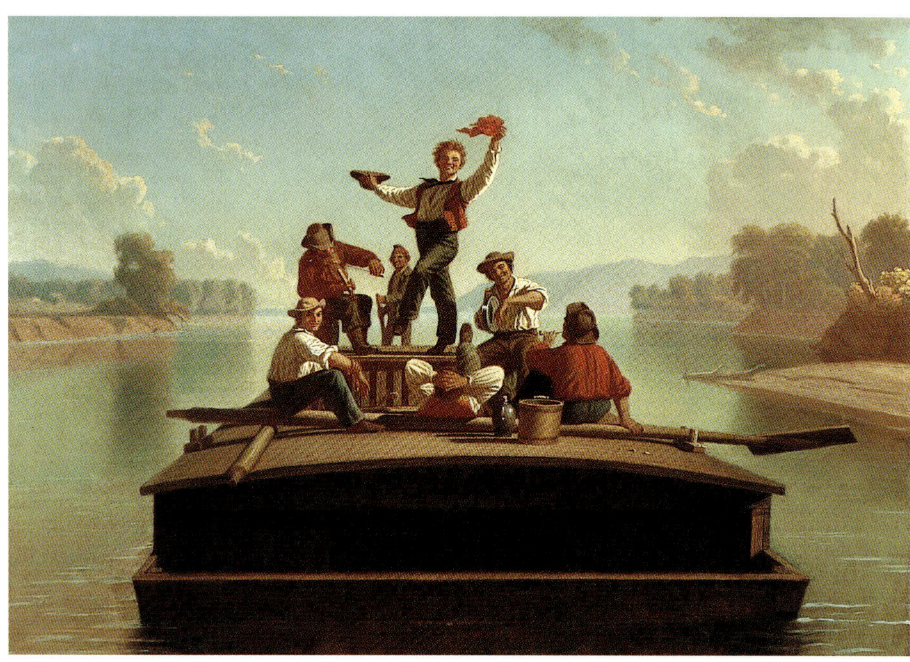

FIG. 44
George Caleb Bingham, ***The Jolly Flatboatmen***,
1877–78.
Oil on canvas, 26 1/16 × 36 3/8 in.
Terra Foundation for the Arts, Daniel J. Terra Collection, 1992.15.
Photograph courtesy of Terra Foundation for the Arts, Chicago.

at auction for one of George Caleb Bingham's *Jolly Flatboatmen* (fig. 44), the record for any American painting to that date.[67] Capitalizing on the interest in *The Icebergs*, Sotheby's borrowed space in the gallery next door to the sales room, then at 980 Madison Avenue. For the sales previews, *The Icebergs* was flanked by a group of smaller landscapes in the same sale; due to the weight of the framed painting (approximately 500 pounds),[68] it rested on a ledge, dramatically lit by spotlights (fig. 14).

On October 25, 1979, John L. Marion took the podium at Sotheby's (fig. 45). The sales room was packed. *The Icebergs* was lot 34 in the sale, estimated at $750,000 to $1 million. If it reached $1 million, *The Icebergs* would break the existing record for an American painting. Marion started the bidding at $500,000. At least eight bidders were active at the $1 million mark, causing ripples of excitement in the sales room.

Taking their time were two telephone bidders. Linda Silverman, then head of contemporary art at Sotheby's, had one client on the line, while Roberta Louckx, from Sotheby's Private Client Services, called another in Dallas. Both bidders had insisted on complete anonymity. As bidding approached $2 million, these two absentees engaged in an excruciatingly tense horserace. Bidding remained at $50,000 increments, and there were generous pauses between each record-breaking bid. Finally, at $2.4 million, Marion pushed the bidding increment to $100,000. With the subsequent and final bid, it took 3 minutes and 45 seconds to reach the hammer price of $2.5 million. Applause erupted as the news sank in. The previous record had been shattered.[69]

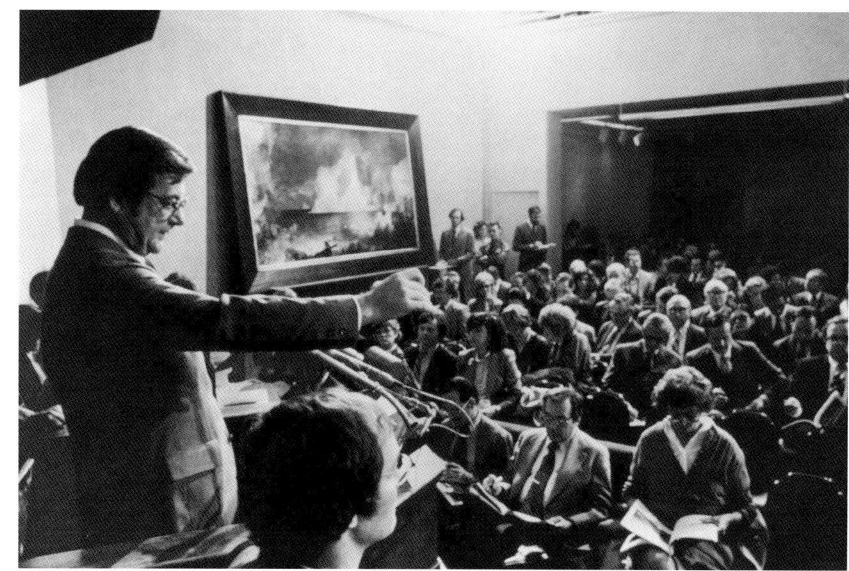

FIG. 45
John L. Marion, chairman of Sotheby Parke Bernet, New York, auctioning Frederic Edwin Church's ***The Icebergs***, October 1979.
Photograph courtesy of Ted Thai/TimePix.

The sale of *The Icebergs* surpassed other benchmarks as well. The previous record for a painting sold in an American auction had been held by Rembrandt's *Aristotle Contemplating the Bust of Homer* (The Metropolitan Museum of Art, New York), which in 1961 had sold for $2.3 million. A personal note attached itself to these sales: John Marion Sr. had been the Sotheby's auctioneer for the sale of the Rembrandt; his son held the gavel as the Church sale eclipsed his father's record. What stunned most observers was that *The Icebergs* achieved the third-highest price paid at auction for any painting, behind the $5.24 million paid for Diego Velázquez's portrait of Juan de Pareja (The Metropolitan Museum of Art, New York) and the $4 million the National Gallery in London paid for Titian's *Death of Actaeon*, both of which had been sold by Christie's in London.[70]

The next day, the *New York Times* gave the sale front-page coverage, including a photograph of the painting and the headline "U.S. Painting Sold for Record $2.5 Million." Speculation as to the identities of the two telephone bidders was rampant. Rumors that Paul Mellon had been interested in the painting for the National Gallery of Art, that the painting was destined for the White House, or that Norton Simon had purchased it for his museum in California were all just that.[71]

The identity of the purchasers of *The Icebergs* has been a subject of speculation since then, but the Dallas Museum of Art has remained true to the buyers' wish for anonymity. The identity of the underbidder has also been a closely held secret until now. Francois de Menil, a talented architect and son of Dominique de Menil, founder of the Menil Collection in Houston, is well known for his interest in contemporary art. But a few days before the auction, he had called Linda Silverman and asked her to handle his bidding for *The Icebergs*.[72] The second runner-up was the celebrated collector

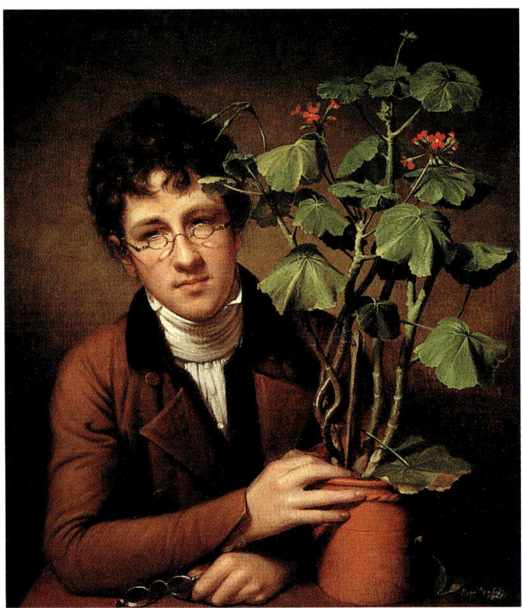

FIG. 46
Rembrandt Peale, ***Rubens Peale with a Geranium***, 1801.
Oil on canvas, 28⅛ × 24 in.
Patrons' Permanent Fund.
Photograph © 2001 Board of Trustees, National Gallery of Art, Washington, D.C.

of American art Daniel J. Terra, bidding through Berry-Hill Galleries in New York. He had set his upper limit at $2 million. The auction's outcome remained a sore spot for him for years.[73]

In Manchester the initial shocked delight over the price realized soon gave way to inevitable internal disputes over how the money should be spent. Not surprisingly, most of the money went to the city of Manchester. The city council eventually purchased the dilapidated country property Mair Baulch had wanted when she first considered selling *The Icebergs*.[74] Following the sale, in 1983, the Charity Commissioners filed suit to see if the courts would uphold the original gift of *The Icebergs* to St. Wilfred's Church; that suit was denied.[75]

In New York and London, the sale of *The Icebergs* generated a similar shock wave. If a painting by Church could come close to the price paid for a work by Titian or Velázquez, what, then, would a Cézanne or a Renoir bring? Collectors, dealers, and auction houses all recalibrated their estimates, using *The Icebergs* as a benchmark. By the spring of 1980, after the next round of European paintings sales, *The Icebergs* had dropped to eleventh on the all-time list of prices paid at auction for paintings.[76] In American art, the auction record set by *The Icebergs* would stand until 1985, when the National Gallery of Art purchased Rembrandt Peale's *Rubens Peale with a Geranium* (fig. 46) for $3.7 million.[77]

David Huntington was obviously pleased with the overwhelming success of the sale of *The Icebergs*; however, he was also concerned about the anonymity of the winning bidder. As a scholar, he feared that the painting, so newly rediscovered, might disappear once again into private hands. But he did not have to wait long before rumors out of Texas suggested the painting was in Dallas and would be placed on long-term loan at the Dallas Museum of Fine Arts (DMFA; the museum shortened its name in 1984).

Huntington was not the only one taken by surprise at the news. Harry S. Parker III, then the director of the DMFA, had been in New York during the sales week and had looked at *The Icebergs* in the company of several museum trustees. They were there for various events, including a meeting with Edward Larrabee Barnes, the proposed architect for the museum's new building in downtown Dallas.[78] In one of many moments of irony during that week, Parker and his party were leaving the restaurant La Grenouille, where they had had lunch, when they saw the eventual buyers of the painting. After exchanging pleasantries, Parker asked if they had seen *The Icebergs* and recommended it to them if they had not. He had no idea whether he had struck a chord or if this chance encounter might have had any influence on their decision to bid on the painting.[79]

The couple who did buy *The Icebergs* were in New York that week on other business but had attended the sales previews and visited several galleries. Standing in front of the painting, they decided to bid on it, knowing it was not a work of art that would fit comfortably in their home. They realized that *The Icebergs* was a museum picture and could have a transforming impact on the DMFA's collection. They spent considerable time in front of the painting, clearly enchanted by it.[80]

With this in mind, they made arrangements to bid by phone, because they would be back in Texas on the day of the sale. Those plans nearly went awry when the bidding started before Louckx was able to get them on the phone, but the slow pace of the sale worked to their advantage.[81]

Transporting the painting to Dallas proved to be a problem as well. The shipper wrote "household items" on the crate to deflect attention from its contents. The ploy was too successful; the crate was bumped from its intended flight and sat in its container on the airport tarmac for a day.[82] Finally, *The Icebergs* arrived safely in Dallas.

Parker had no idea who had purchased *The Icebergs* until the week following the sale. The purchasers called him to request a few minutes of his time on a matter, they said, that Parker might find worth his while. Would Parker be interested in having *The Icebergs* on loan at the Museum? There was one restriction: that the lenders be permitted to remain anonymous. Museum personnel would agree not to confirm, deny, or speculate as to the lenders' identity. This remains the greatest surprise of Parker's twenty-eight years as a museum director. Indeed, as the couple sat in his office in Dallas, he had the distinct impression they were enjoying the moment as much as he was. Throughout the discussions surrounding the eventual donation of *The Icebergs,* those who came into contact with the buyers share a common perception of a couple uninterested in personal accolades, with no desire for the spotlight, but a genuine commitment to philanthropy.

About the same time, *The Icebergs'* new owners made one other call, to Kennedy Galleries in New York, to buy the chromolithograph of *The Icebergs*—which they had seen during their visit the previous week—for 1/100th the price of the oil painting. Their rationale was simple: if they could not keep the painting, they would enjoy owning the print.[83]

The dinner-party buzz in Dallas had also picked up on the rumor that *The Icebergs* was headed to Texas. Gerald L. Carr was then a professor of art history at Southern Methodist University (SMU) in Dallas. Knowing of Carr's interest in Frederic Church, William B. Jordan, then director of the Meadows Museum at SMU, passed along the news. His timing was impeccable. Within hours, Parker called Carr to ask if he would write a book chronicling the history of the painting for an exhibition scheduled for the fall of 1980.[84]

Parker had one more hurdle to jump before any of this could become public knowledge. The DMFA was facing a tough bond election in early November, the outcome of which would determine if the Museum could afford to move from its cramped but historically significant quarters on the Texas Centennial Fair Grounds to a desirable site in the heart of the newly designated downtown Arts District. Concerned that a splashy announcement might derail support for the bond issue, Parker decided to delay the unveiling of *The Icebergs* until after the election.[85] The bond issue passed, and the following day, November 7, the DMFA issued a press release announcing the arrival of *The Icebergs* on long-term loan to the collection. The Museum scheduled previews for the Dallas City Council, upper-level members of the Museum, and the press and presented the painting to the public on Tuesday, November 20. What no one knew until the unveiling of the painting was that the purchasers were not just lending, but donating *The Icebergs* to the Museum. That gesture was, and remains, an unparalleled act of personal and civic generosity.

The Icebergs then made a series of appearances, much as it had in the 1860s: first in Dallas, then in Washington, D.C., as part of the National Gallery of Art's landmark exhibition *American Light*. That exhibition and catalogue encouraged the appreciation of American landscape painting and reaffirmed the importance of Hudson River School landscapes in public and private American art collections. In the fall of 1980 *The Icebergs*, newly cleaned and home from its twentieth-century debuts, was the focus of a solo exhibition at the DMFA (fig. 15), organized by the Museum and with a monograph prepared by Carr and Huntington. The event gave Museum visitors and scholars the opportunity to admire the long-lost painting and appreciate its story as recounted in the accompanying book.

The donation of *The Icebergs* had an immediate effect on Dallas and the Museum, quite apart from the incessant desire to learn the donors' identity. As Parker noted in the press release announcing the loan of *The Icebergs*, "It signals confidence in the cultural future of our Museum as an increasingly major institution. We have been working hard on the American collection to achieve a high level cross-section of the art tradition of our country. Now this collection will have a centerpiece and the people of Dallas will have access on a continuing basis to a great work of art."[86] It turned the art world's attention to Dallas as the city's museum moved up in the estimation of many museum colleagues and as it made plans to move into a new facility. For Huntington, it justified his long-held faith that this lost painting would reappear. For the painting's donors, it provided immense personal pleasure to know that they had brought a great painting, and a great story, to Dallas. *The Icebergs* had come a long way, from an artist's "white elephant" to the centerpiece of a museum collection. For the Dallas Museum of Art, *The Icebergs* remains now, as it was in 1979, a symbol of civic philanthropy and proof of the enduring power of a great painting.

Notes

1. On some occasions Church arranged for a more extensive tour of cities in both the United States and Great Britain. For an annual account of Church's exhibitions, see the Chronology in Franklin Kelly et al., *Frederic Edwin Church* (Washington, D.C.: National Gallery of Art, 1989), 158–71.

2. Williams, Stevens, Williams & Co., New York, published a pamphlet titled *Church's Painting of Nature's Grandest Scene. Niagara, The Great Fall. By Frederic Edward* [sic] *Church* in 1857 as part of the subscription form for the chromolithograph of *Niagara* (Corcoran Gallery of Art Archives, Washington, D.C.). The brochure included excerpts from six laudatory reviews of the painting when it made its debut in May 1857. My thanks to Marisa Keller, Archivist, Corcoran Gallery of Art, for this information. Two years later, Theodore Winthrop wrote *A Companion to The Heart of the Andes* (New York: D. Appleton and Co., 1859), and Louis Legrand Noble wrote the pamphlet *Church's Painting. The Heart of the Andes* (New York: D. Appleton and Co., 1859), interpreting that painting for viewers.

3. Gerald L. Carr, introduction by David C. Huntington, *Frederic Edwin Church: The Icebergs* (Dallas: Dallas Museum of Fine Arts and University of Texas Press, 1980), is the most comprehensive treatment of the history of this painting. Taken together with his article "Beyond the Tip: Some Addenda to Frederic Church's 'The Icebergs,'" *Arts* 56, no. 3 (November 1981): 107–11, and his chapter on the Arctic in his *In Search of the Promised Land: Paintings by Frederic Edwin Church* (New York: Berry-Hill Galleries; Hanover, N.H.: University Press of New England, 2000), Carr has impressively mapped the evolution and significance of this painting. I am indebted to his scholarship and friendship for the writing of this essay.

4. See Eleanor Jones Harvey, "The Artistic Conquest of the Far North," in *Cosmos: From Romanticism to Avant-Garde*, ed. Jean Clair et al. (Montreal: Montreal Museum of Fine Arts; New York: Prestel Verlag, 1999), 108–13.

5. See Carr, *In Search of the Promised Land*, 80.

6. Louis Legrand Noble, *After Icebergs with a Painter: A Summer Voyage to Labrador and around Newfoundland* (New York and London, 1861; reprint, New York: Olana Galleries, 1979), 127.

7. Ibid., 108.

8. [Louis L. Noble], "The Iceberg of Torbay," *Atlantic Monthly* 6 (October 1860): 443–48. Church was evidently complicit in the publication of this unattributed excerpt from Noble's forthcoming book; see Carr, "Beyond the Tip," 108.

9. Henry W. French, *Art and Artists in Connecticut* (New York: Charles T. Dillingham, 1879), 130.

10. The original exhibition dates were April 24–June 22, 1861. Carr notes that the exhibition appears to have been extended through July 9, 1861, based on daily notices in the "Amusements This Evening" listings found on the editorial pages of the *New York Times* through that date; see Carr, "Beyond the Tip," 107.

11. Early press reports variously called the work in progress *The Icebergs, The Icebergs at Noon-Day, View in the Arctic Region*, and *Crown of the Arctic Regions*; see Carr, *The Icebergs*, 72.

12. The Rev. Theodore L. Cuyler, "Among the Icebergs," *Independent* (New York), May 2, 1861, 1. Gerald Carr recently discovered a more extensively descriptive review, printed in this volume on page 92.

13. *New-York Daily Tribune*, April 24, 1861.

14. *Boston Daily Evening Transcript*, May 27, 1861, remarked, "One hardly knows what to say about it. . . . After a while, however, you get into the picture, so to speak; and the panoramic berg begins to tell its story to your curious and admiring gaze." The *World* noted on April 29, 1861, "We think it will require some time to get even on speaking terms with the 'Icebergs.' They are not to be taken into the soul with a glance." *Harper's Weekly* of April 24, 1861, called the work "as bold a picture as ever was painted, for there is nothing before you but air, light, and water." All citations appear in Carr, *The Icebergs*, 83, 73.

15. "Fine Arts. Mr. Church among the Icebergs," *Albion* (New York), May 4, 1861, 213.

16. Hayes was also a member of the Geographical Society. He had previously served under the famous Arctic explorer Elisha Kent Kane (1820–1857); see *Cosmos*. For a thorough and accessible history of Arctic exploration, see Pierre Berton, *The Arctic Grail: The Quest for the North West Passage and the North Pole, 1818–1909* (New York: Viking, 1988).

17. Quoted in the *New York Times*, November 15, 1861, 3; cited in Carr, "Beyond the Tip," 109.

18. Americans were not the only ones to probe the relevance of *The North* to the ongoing conflict. Considering Noble's *After Icebergs with a Painter*, a British reviewer seized on a passage in the book that describes the relationship between Britain and America (colloquially known as "John Bull" and "Brother Jonathan"). Noble had written, "In fact Jonathan is a youth only, and John an old man. When the lad gets his growth he will be everywhere, and the old fogy by that time comparatively nowhere." To which the reviewer then observed, "But

what if Jonathan splits asunder like a shattered iceberg!—what if the Northern and Southern sides rend asunder with a fearful crash, while the 'old fogy' continues unmoved as a mountain!" See "After Icebergs with a Painter: A Summer Voyage to Labrador and around Newfoundland, by Rev. Louis L. Noble (Low & Co.)," *The Athenaeum*, no. 1769 (September 21, 1861): 370.

19. Carr, *In Search of the Promised Land*, 83.

20. Specifically, Church's composition recalls the English painter Stephen Pearce's (1819–1904) panoply of Arctic explorer portraits owned by the National Portrait Gallery, London.

21. "Fine Arts. Church's New Pictures," *Illustrated London News* 47, no. 1323 (July 8, 1865): 18; courtesy Sandra Feldman. See also William H. Truettner, "The Genesis of Frederic Edwin Church's *Aurora Borealis*," *Art Quarterly* 31 (autumn 1968): 267–83.

22. David C. Huntington, *The Landscapes of Frederic Edwin Church: Vision of an American Era* (New York: George Braziller, 1966), 86.

23. The London exhibition dates were June 22–September 19, 1863.

24. *Court Journal* (London), June 27, 1863, 633; noted in Carr, *The Icebergs*, 88. Sir George Back (1798–1874) explored the Arctic region in 1833. Lady Jane Franklin (1792–1875) was the widow of Sir John Franklin. McClintock (1819–1907), Rae (1813–1893), Belcher (1799–1877), and Collinson (1811–1877) all made voyages in search of Franklin during the 1850s. Tyndall (1820–1893) was a renowned physicist and natural philosopher who specialized in understanding the earth's periods of glaciation.

25. "A National Gallery of Paintings," *Boston Daily Evening Transcript*, January 17, 1865; cited in Carr, "Beyond the Tip," 110.

26. Letter from Omer Lavallée, Corporate Archivist, Canadian Pacific, to Sandra Feldman, July 29, 1977; letter courtesy Sandra Feldman.

27. In 1861 Watkin traveled to Canada to untangle financial problems associated with the consolidation of several railroad companies. The duke of Newcastle, who was also secretary of state for the British colonies in North America, requested that Watkin serve as his confidential agent on that trip, to determine the feasibility of bringing the then separate colonies into confederation as a single country under British rule. On July 1, 1867, Ontario, Quebec, Nova Scotia, and New Brunswick became the founding provinces of modern-day Canada. The remaining British colonies and territories joined the dominion between 1870 and 1949. See George Smith, *The Dictionary of National Biography, Supplement* (January 1901–December 1911, edited by Sir Sidney Lee), vol. 1, *Abbey–Eyre* (Oxford: Oxford University Press, 1912), 602; citation courtesy Sandra Feldman.

28. "Farewell Banquet," *New York Times*, October 31, 1865, 1; cited in Gerald L. Carr, "Albert Bierstadt, Big Trees, and the British: A Log of Many Anglo-American Ties," *Arts* 60, no. 10 (summer 1986): 60.

29. "Dinner to Professor Longfellow," unidentified clipping from a British newspaper, Bierstadt family scrapbook, Joyce Randall Edwards Collection, Dobbs Ferry, N.Y.; copy courtesy Sandra Feldman. According to Esther Osborne (sister of Bierstadt's wife, Rosalie), Watkin was among the visitors to Bierstadt's country home and studio, Malkasten; cited in Carr, "Log," 64.

30. *London Evening News and Post*, December 7, 1891, 2; quoted in Carr, *In Search of the Promised Land*, 83.

31. Watkin obituary: "Services in His Younger Days to Manchester," unidentified English newspaper, April 20, 1901, and "Sir Edward Watkin, M.P., at Northenden," *Hythe and Sandgate Echo*, October 22, 1881; citations courtesy Sandra Feldman.

32. "Our Third Chairman: Sir Edward W. Watkin, Bart., M.P.," *Great Central Railway Journal* 3, no. 6 (December 1907): 119; citation courtesy Sandra Feldman.

33. Watkin first petitioned to dig such a tunnel in 1869. "Our Album: Sir Edward William Watkin, Knight, M.P., the Railway King," *MOMUS*, November 13, 1879, 81; citation courtesy Sandra Feldman.

34. Sir E. W. Watkin, *Canada and the States: Recollections, 1851–1886* (London and New York: Warwick & Co., 1887), 511–12; citation courtesy Sandra Feldman. This passage is also quoted in part in Carr, *The Icebergs*, 96.

35. Watkin, *Canada and the States: Recollections*, vii; quoted in Carr, *The Icebergs*, 96.

36. "Fine Arts. Church's New Pictures," *Illustrated London News* 47, no. 1323 (July 8, 1865): 18; "Mr. F. E. Church's New Pictures," unidentified British clipping, 1865, New York Public Library Artist Archives; and W. P. Bayley, "Mr. Church's Pictures. 'Cotopaxi,' 'Chimborazo,' and 'The Aurora Borealis.' Considered with Reference to English Art," *London Art-Journal* 4 (September 1, 1865): 265.

37. At first Weimann was unable to find a buyer, as the painting's high-keyed palette deterred would-be owners from paying the $35,000 asking price. Eventually Sherman Lee, director of the Cleveland Museum of Art, saw the painting in the conservation laboratory at the Fogg Art Museum at Harvard University and purchased it for Cleveland. Telephone conversations with American art collector Arthur Jay Phelan, September 16, 2001, and Christopher Weimann, son of the late Robert Weimann, November 26, 2001.

38. Henry Tuckerman, *Book of the Artists: American Artist Life* (New York: G. P. Putnam & Son, 1867), 384.

39. Frank J. Bonelle, "In Summer Time on Olana: Grand Views of the Hudson River and the Catskills," *Boston Sunday Herald*, September 7, 1890, 17.

40. Telephone conversation with Christopher Weimann, November 26, 2001.

41. Telephone conversations with Trudy Huntington, widow of David C. Huntington, November 28, 2001, and Jay Phelan, September 16, 2001.

42. This essay could not have been realized without the generous help of Sandra Feldman, then a researcher with Hirschl & Adler Galleries, Inc., New York. Her files include all of the leads, blind alleys, correspondence, and notes from her two years of research. I am grateful to her for sharing so much of her time and information with me.

43. Telephone conversation with Sandra Feldman on November 6, 2001; conversation with Stuart Feld, November 8, 2001; telephone conversation with Jay Maroney, November 6, 2001.

44. Feldman found references to Watkin in the Bierstadt family scrapbook, an invaluable resource for her work on *Mt. Rosalie* (see n. 29). Perusing a copy of the *Dictionary of National Biography* in a London bookstore, she came across mention of Watkin's travel memoirs, all of which solidified her identification of Watkin as the original owner of *The Icebergs* (see n. 27).

45. Watkin, *Canada and the States*, 511–12.

46. A trip to Folkestone's library and train station yielded no clues; a visit to his former address there (since converted to a set of flats) netted her an audience with its current resident, the former French consul to Beverly Hills, California. This yielded a fascinating conversation about Zsa Zsa Gabor, an acquaintance of the consul's, but no information on Watkin. Feldman and her host did check behind the newer walls subdividing the original structure to see if the painting might have been left there, but to no avail. Telephone conversation with Sandra Feldman, November 6, 2001.

47. "The 1m-Dollar 'Dartboard,'" *Manchester Evening News*, July 6, 1979, A1; Donald Wintersgill, "Plans for Fund from Sale of Picture," *Manchester Guardian*, November 23, 1979; Malcolm Edis, "Highly Rated Work," *Local Government Chronicle*, May 6, 1983, 498. Although there were rumors that Rose Hill's charges had thrown darts at *The Icebergs*, this was not the case, as Sotheby's conservation report of 1979 makes clear. Conservation report courtesy Sotheby's, copy in the DMA curatorial files.

48. There is precedent for this, including the National Gallery of Art's version of Thomas Cole's series, *The Voyage of Life*. That set of four paintings was conveyed with the sale of the house, sold in 1908 by the heirs of the original owner. The house became the Bethesda Hospital and Deaconess Association of the Methodist Church of Cincinnati, and the paintings remained there until 1971. Conversation with Stuart Feld, November 8, 2001, and telephone conversation with Franklin Kelly, Curator of British and American Paintings, National Gallery of Art, December 5, 2001.

49. Mr. D. Taylor, Local History Librarian, City of Manchester Cultural Services, made Rose Hill sound more like a prison than a halfway house. Conversation with Sandra Feldman, November 8, 2001.

50. Ibid.

51. Sandra Feldman to Mr. D. Taylor, May 31, 1978; letter courtesy Sandra Feldman.

52. Mr. D. Taylor, to Sandra Feldman, June 7, 1978; letter courtesy Sandra Feldman.

53. "A $2.5 Million Find," *Newsweek*, November 5, 1979. Conversations with Gerald Carr, November 2 and 9, 2001, and telephone conversation with Mair Baulch, November 26, 2001.

54. Telephone conversations with James Miller, Sotheby's London, November 19, and Sir Timothy Clifford, Director-General of the National Galleries of Scotland, November 15, 2001.

55. Telephone conversation with James Miller, November 19, 2001. See also Stanley Goldsmith, "Million Dollar Oil Painting Found in Remand Home," *Manchester Daily Telegraph*, July 7, 1979, 17, which shows a photograph of Clifford standing next to the painting.

56. Telephone conversation with Sir Timothy Clifford, November 15, 2001.

57. Telephone conversation with Grete Meilman, October 29, 2001. I am indebted to Meilman, then co-chair of the American paintings department, Sotheby's New York, for her enthusiastic support of this project and her willingness to share her time and expertise in reconstructing Sotheby's part in the rediscovery of *The Icebergs*.

58. Conversation with Grete Meilman and Peter Rathbone, then co-chair and now head of the American paintings department, Sotheby's New York, November 8, 2001.

59. "The 1m-Dollar 'Dartboard'"; Stanley Goldsmith, "Million Dollar Oil Painting Found in Remand Home," *Manchester Daily Telegraph*, July 7, 1979.

60. Conversations with Stuart Feld, of Hirschl & Adler, and Sandra Feldman, November 8, 2001.

61. Conversation with Peter Rathbone and Grete Meilman, November 8, 2001.

62. The April 1915 issue of the parish magazine announced Parkyn's gift of *The Icebergs* to the newly opened church rooms. The painting was returned to Rose Hill in 1921 after a troupe of actors performing *As You Like It* in the church hall complained that it was in their way. Charles H. Royle to James MacDonald, Esq., June 10, 1921. The letter accepting the painting back is dated June 22, 1921. Copies of both letters were sent by Greg Forster, Rector, Northenden Rectory, St. Wilfred's Church, Manchester, to John Lunsford, DMFA Senior Curator, January 8, 1980; DMA curatorial files. This story was recounted in [Daily Telegraph Reporter], "Council Can Keep £1m from Painting," *London Daily Telegraph*, March 8, 1983.

63. Laurie Johnston, "2 Britons Find U.S. Artist's Long-Lost 'Icebergs,'" *New York Times*, August 17, 1979, B1.

64. According to Peter Rathbone, this painting was brought for evaluation to a Sotheby's Heirloom Discovery Day. Conversation with Peter Rathbone, November 8, 2001. The painting sold in Sotheby's American paintings sale on October 27, 1978, lot 23.

65. *The Hudson Bay Looking across the Tappan Zee*, 1866, private collection. Sold in Sotheby's American paintings sale, October 31, 1975, lot 30.

66. *Still Life with Violin*, dated 1885. Sold in Sotheby's American paintings sale, April 20, 1979, lot 16A.

67. *Jolly Flatboatmen, No. 2* sold in Sotheby's American paintings sale, June 6, 1978, lot 549. Roughly six months later, Daniel J. Terra, a leading collector of American art, purchased the painting. The painting is now in the collection of the Terra Museum of American Art, Chicago.

68. Church affixed *The Icebergs* to a solid, panel-back oak stretcher, which would have weighed close to 250 pounds with the painted canvas. The present mahogany frame, found at Rose Hill, weighs an additional 250 pounds. I am grateful to Ross Merrill, Chief of Conservation at the National Gallery of Art, Washington, D.C., for help with these calculations.

69. All information from Rita Reif, "U.S. Painting Sold for Record $2.5 Million," *New York Times*, October 26, 1979, A1, C22.

70. The Velázquez sold for $5.24 million, plus commission, on January 27, 1970, lot 110; the Titian sold for $3.84 million on June 25, 1971, lot 27.

71. Paul Richard, "Tips on 'The Icebergs': The Long-Lost Canvas, on Loan to Dallas," *Washington Post*, November 7, 1979, Style sec., B1, B8.

72. Telephone conversations with Linda Silverman, November 8, 2001, and Francois de Menil, November 20, 2001.

73. Conversation with Fred Hill and James Hill, Berry-Hill Galleries, November 9, 2001.

74. Within a few years, the Baulches retired, and during a nationwide reorganization of Social Services, Rose Hill was closed as a remand center, and the house and grounds were sold for development. However, Rose Hill is on the English Heritage register, and the developer has promised to restore the ancestral home as a set of executive flats. That work remains to be done. Telephone conversations with Greg Forster, November 19, 2001; Sir Timothy Clifford, November 15, 2001; and Glen and Mair Baulch, November 26, 2001.

75. Malcolm Edis, "Highly Rated Work," *Local Government Chronicle*, May 6, 1983, 498–99, and correspondence from Malcolm Edis, Principal Solicitor, City of Manchester, dated May 11, 1983; DMA curatorial files. Telephone conversation with Greg Forster, November 19, 2001.

76. Christie's New York, *Ten Important Pictures from the Collection of Henry Ford II*, May 13, 1980. The roster of artists included Edouard Manet, Paul Cézanne, Pierre-Auguste Renoir, Vincent van Gogh, Edgar Degas, Pablo Picasso, Amedeo Modigliani, and Eugène Boudin.

77. Sotheby's American paintings sale, December 5, 1985, lot 42.

78. DMFA Director's files.

79. Telephone conversation with Harry Parker, November 15, 2001.

80. Telephone conversation with John Marion, November 15, 2001.

81. Telephone conversation with Roberta Louckx, Sotheby's Private Client Services, November 14, 2001.

82. Ibid.

83. Conversation with the donors, November 6, 2001.

84. Telephone conversations with Gerald Carr, November 2, 2001, and Harry Parker, November 15, 2001.

85. Telephone conversation with Harry Parker, November 15, 2001; see also Richard, "Tips on 'The Icebergs,'" B1, B8.

86. DMFA press release, November 7, 1979. DMA curatorial files.

Gerald L. Carr

EARLY DOCUMENTATION OF *THE ICEBERGS*

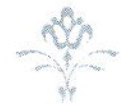

Archival Sources

Frederic Edwin Church to Captain William Knight, 15 Tenth St., New York, October 7, 1859. Private collection, Canada.

"I have just received the Walrus Head for which please receive many thanks—it is a great curiosity—the Orion sails tomorrow and I have just had time to order a package of colours paper &c to be sent on board for you I hope that they will reach you in good order—

Rough paper is prepared for Oil colours—Mr. Noble is engaged in writing an account of our trip I have not seen him for some time—as he lives out of the city—he would be glad to be remembered to you if he knew I was writing.

Will you be kind enough to inform Mr. Newman that I have just received a package of letters from St. John's. I shall be glad to hear from you at any time and of your progress in sketching icebergs. Many thanks for your kind offer regarding the Deer Horns."

W. P. Bayley to Church, 6 Durham Terrace Westbourne Park, London, March 2, 1860. Frederic Edwin Church, Letters and Diaries, David C. Huntington Archives, Olana State Historic Site, New York State Office of Parks, Recreation and Historic Preservation (Olana Archives).

"There are many here who look forward with no ordinary interest for the next work which we hope you may feel disposed to send us. It has been said here that you were last summer [1859] in the northern seas running tilt with your adventurous pencil against some tremendous iceberg—If so, it is a matter of earnest congratulation to find that you have been safely wintering in New York once more."

Church to Theodore Winthrop, New York, March 16, 1860. Manuscripts and Archives Division, New York Public Library, Ford Collection.

". . . If I am interrupted now—I shall very probably be obliged to give up attempting the Icebergs until next winter[,] which will be a serious damage because I wished to commence it this season and after getting it fairly started lay it by for the summer months in order that I might see it with refreshed eyes next season—"

Church to unknown addressee, New York, April 24, 1860. Manuscripts and Special Services Division, New York State Library, Albany.

". . . Mr Noble has heard nothing from the 'Atlantic Monthly' people whatever—"

John McClure to Church, McKeand's 46 Clark St, Chicago, January 19, 1860. David C. Huntington Archives, Olana State Historic Site, New York State Office of Parks, Recreation and Historic Preservation (Olana Archives).

". . . I long to hear how the Icebergs get on—I hope you still think you will finish them by the time you expected. From present indications there is every appearance of a lively spring trade in New York, whether the Cotton States stay out in the cold or not."

John McClure to Church, McKeand's 46 Clark St, Chicago, Feb[y] 2, 1861. David C. Huntington Archives, Olana State Historic Site, New York State Office of Parks, Recreation and Historic Preservation (Olana Archives).

". . . I am delighted to hear such favorable reports of the 'Icebergs' and sympathize with your difficulties—that you will overcome them all successfully I have no doubt. Try and hit the London season this time, according to accounts it will be a stirring one for art."

John McClure to Church, Chicago, February 19, 1861. David C. Huntington Archives, Olana State Historic Site, New York State Office of Parks, Recreation and Historic Preservation (Olana Archives).

McClure writes that Bayard Taylor, in lectures on baron von Humboldt, mentions Church's *Heart of the Andes* and adds that Mrs. Bayard Taylor is enthusiastic about *The Icebergs*.

John McClure to Church, St. Louis Academy of Fine Art, March 1, 1861. David C. Huntington Archives, Olana State Historic Site, New York State Office of Parks, Recreation and Historic Preservation (Olana Archives).

Concerning exhibition arrangements for *The Icebergs*: "I trust it will be of such a nature as not to interfere with any arrangement between yourself and me which may be deemed necessary to make. . . . I am glad to see you write so cheery [*sic*] about the progress of the Icebergs—I long to see it—You do well to let as few as possible see it. . . . I can't help hoping gold will do best for the [frame of the] 'Icebergs.'"

John McClure to Church, St. Louis, March 5, 1861. David C. Huntington Archives, Olana State Historic Site, New York State Office of Parks, Recreation and Historic Preservation (Olana Archives).

McClure hopes to share a viewing of *The Icebergs* "and your *very* best cup of chocolate" with Church, the following Wednesday.

Joseph Church to Church, Hartford, March 14, 1861. David C. Huntington Archives, Olana State Historic Site, New York State Office of Parks, Recreation and Historic Preservation (Olana Archives).

". . . I am very glad that you are likely to succeed so well with your picture [*The Icebergs*]. . . . I hope you will place it in such hands as to receive something from it. It now appears you will need it—I have never been able to learn that you received any thing from the two last large pictures [*Niagara* and *The Heart of the Andes*] Except the sale of them."

George Templeton Strong, diary entry for March 14, 1861, The New-York Historical Society. Published in *The Diary of George Templeton Strong*, ed. Alan Nevins, 3 vols. (New York: Macmillan, 1952), 3:110.

John McClure to Church, 100 Buchanan St., Glasgow [Scotland], August 1, 1861. David C. Huntington Archives, Olana State Historic Site, New York State Office of Parks, Recreation and Historic Preservation (Olana Archives).

". . . I find business is even more seriously affected here by American troubles than I expected. I was in London for a week and never in my life knew things so dull[,] the fine art world is of course most seriously influenced, and the great publishers are doing nothing. I assure you I feel very thankful the 'Iceberg' picture was not brought over."

John McClure to Church, New York, July 15, 1862. David C. Huntington Archives, Olana State Historic Site, New York State Office of Parks, Recreation and Historic Preservation (Olana Archives).

". . . I shall write to Mr Humphrey tomorrow it would be useless to show the 'Icebergs' in Rochester at present. . . ."

John McClure to Church, New York City, September 29, 1862. David C. Huntington Archives, Olana State Historic Site, New York State Office of Parks, Recreation and Historic Preservation (Olana Archives).

". . . I am glad you have written Mr Roberts offering him the use of the 'Icebergs.'"

Notices of The Icebergs *in Progress*

"An Artist Hunt for Icebergs." *Pennsylvania Inquirer and National Gazette*, June 21, 1859.

"An artist hunt for icebergs. Mr. Church, who has so superbly painted Niagara and the Andes, has gone to Halifax, in company with Cole's biographer, the Rev. Louis L. Noble, whence they will cruise off the Newfoundland Banks for icebergs, which Mr. Cole [*sic*] intends to sketch for a new picture. This is quite an adventure on the part of Mr. Church and his friend, as they may find, if they should come too suddenly into the presence of these stately monsters of the deep. Nothing is more dangerous than floating ice, when it is moving under the action of a current. The vast sweep it has—the force with which thousands of tons close in upon a vessel, can only be appreciated by those whose lives have been imperilled by its slow and majestic power. Mr. Church has a great subject before him; and if he can convey by a picture the real character of fields or mountains of moving ice, as he has that of Niagara, and, as it is said, of the Andes, he will add another leaf to his growing laurels."

"An Artist Hunt for Icebergs." *Boston Daily Evening Transcript*, June 23, 1859, 1.

Acknowledged reprint of the *Pennsylvania Inquirer* story.

"Personal." *New-York Daily Tribune*, June 25, 1859, 5.

Unacknowledged digest of the *Pennsylvania Inquirer* story.

New York Morning Express, June 27, 1859, 2.

Evangelist (New York), June 30, 1859, 5.

Home Journal (New York), July 2, 1859, 2.

"Personal." *New York Evening Post*, August 5, 1859, 2.

Further reports of August and September 1859, led by this one, noted that the artist, having accomplished his mission, was headed home:

"Church, the painter, having put on canvass Niagara and the Andes, is now essaying the icebergs. He was met on the coast of Labrador last month, where the supply of icebergs had been larger and finer than at any previous season, having completed over a hundred sketches in color of these Arctic monsters. So we may in time expect the Heart of the Icebergs, if these cold and glittering piles can be said to have a heart."

Boston Daily Evening Transcript, August 6, 1859, 2.

New-York Commercial Advertiser, August 6, 1859, 2.

New York Daily News, August 6, 1859, 4.

New-York Daily Tribune, August 6, 1859, 5.

New York Morning Express, August 8, 1859, 2.

Evangelist (New York), August 11, 1859, 5.

Independent (New York), August 11, 1859, 6.

Observer (New York), August 11, 1859, 254.

Cosmopolitan Art Journal (New York), September 1859, 182.

Morning Courier and New-York Enquirer, December 17, 1859, 2.

"Personal." *New York Evening Post*, December 17, 1859, 2.

Reprint of the *Morning Courier* story.

"Art Items." *New-York Daily Tribune*, December 23, 1859, 5.

Notes that Church has "not yet unpacked his Newfoundland Sketches of Icebergs."

New York Leader, December 31, 1859, 3.

"Art Items." *New-York Daily Tribune*, June 9, 1860, 5.

". . . Now, that he has finished this picture [*Twilight in the Wilderness*], he will probably go to work upon his studies of Icebergs, which he brought from Newfoundland last year, and give us a composition of Ocean grandeurs worthy of a companionship with his Niagara, his Heart of the Andes, and his Twilight in the Wilderness."

"Art Items." *World* (New York), July 16, 1860, 2.

Notes that Church would shortly spend "a few weeks" at Mount Desert Island "to make some 'rough water' studies for his 'iceberg' picture, a subject we are glad to know, he intends completing as soon as possible."

"Art Gossip." *Cosmopolitan Art Journal* (New York), September 1860, 126.

"Art." *New York Morning Express*, September 13, 1860, 1.

In September the *New York Express* affirmed that Church, "impatient" after having been injured in an accident at his farm (the future Olana) in upstate New York, had not yet begun the new canvas.

"Literary." *New York Evening Post*, September 20, 1860, 2.

"Literary Items." *Boston Daily Evening Transcript*, September 24, 1860, 4.

"D. Appleton and Co. will shortly publish a charming work entitled 'After Icebergs with a Painter,' written by Rev. Lewis [*sic*] L. Noble, who accompanied Mr. Church on his recent trip to the ice-fields of the North Atlantic to make sketches for his intended picture, of which all our readers have doubtless heard. Mr. Noble is favorably known to the literary world by his 'Life of Cole' and other works."

[Noble, Louis L.]. "'The Iceberg of Torbay.'" *Atlantic Monthly: A Magazine of Literature, Art, and Politics* 6 (October 1860): 443–448.

"Personal." *Home Journal* (New York), October 13, 1860, 2.

Bruno. "Correspondence of the Journal. Art and Artists in New York. New York, Nov. 29, 1860." *Providence (R.I.) Daily Journal*, December 4, 1860, 2.

". . . The [small] canvas with reminiscences of Labrador answers to the sunny scenes of tropic valleys, and the outline of his coming picture—what shall I call it? the Heart of the Icebergs?—looks with cool grandeur and complacency upon the huge drawers that contain warm Ecuadorian landscapes, or Cotopaxi with its livid fire. . . .

CHURCH'S NEXT PAINTING.

The craunching ice-bergs of Labrador will be the next picture which the lovers of art will greet from the hand of Church. His past triumphs are the earnest that this painting—of a subject so new and original—will not fall behind the glowing wonders of the 'Andes' and of 'Niagara.'"

"Personal." *World* (New York), December 7, 1860, 3.

Reprint from *Providence Daily Journal*.

"Gossip about American Artists." *New York Evening Post*, December 11, 1860, 1.

Reprint from *Providence Daily Journal*.

"Art-Gossip." *New York Times* supplement, December 22, 1860, 1.

"Church, having made a name, is crowded with work and annoyed by visitors . . . and is chalking on a large piece, picturing the icebergs, in which he intends spreading both himself and paint to an extent most gratifying to know."

"Art Items." *New-York Daily Tribune*, December 25, 1860, 7.

"Mr. Church has at last commenced upon his undertaking of painting an iceberg, studies for which he made two years ago [*sic*] in Newfoundland. The canvas is the same size as that of the Heart of the Andes. The sole object in the picture will be a vast and solitary iceberg, a mountain of glittering ice, with domes, and fantastical pinancles [*sic*] rising out of the ocean."

"Art Intelligence." *New-York Commercial Advertiser,* January 21, 1861, 2.

"Fine Arts." *New York Herald,* January 23, 1861, 5.

"Sketchings. Domestic Art Gossip." *Crayon* 8 (February 1861): 44.

"Fine Arts." *New York Herald,* February 2, 1861, 2.

"Fine Arts." *New York Evening Post,* February 5, 1861, 1.

Reprint from *Crayon.*

"The Fine Arts." *Providence (R.I.) Daily Journal,* February 21, 1861, 1.

"Art." *New York Evening Express,* February 26, 1861, 1.

"Church is engaged on what is destined to be his greatest production, 'The Icebergs.' This work is still very incomplete, but bears marks of a master's hand; the great originality of the conception is quite equalled by the originality displayed in the treatment. In painting a scene, where only water, in some of its various forms of ice, snow clouds and sea, is represented, many of the ordinary rules of painting are reversed; and the difficulties of the artist are increased by the necessity of finding new methods of accomplishing familiar and technical aims. It is, however, evident even now, that Mr. Church will conquer all technical difficulties; while the magnificence of his imagination has never before been so manifest as in the great masses of ice so strangely grouped, in the wild solitude, the immense distance, and the bleak grandeur, he has already put upon the canvas. In this work, he rises to the rank of a creator."

"Studies of Life. The Studio Building." *New York Leader,* March 9, 1861, 1, 6.

Remarks that, with luck, Church might be induced to "descant upon the majesties of the iceberg" for Studio Building visitors.

"Art Gossip." *New York Times,* March 16, 1861, 2.

"Mr. Church's View in the Arctic Region." *New York Times,* March 29, 1861, 4.

The unsigned author (presumably the *Times*'s editor-in-chief, Henry J. Raymond) remarked admiringly on Church's love of extreme climatic contrasts, the poetic attractions of "ice and snow views" (to be traced back, according to the writer, verbally to the Book of Job and visually to paintings by the late-sixteenth–early-seventeenth-century Flemish artist Joos de Momper), the kindred sentiments of Samuel Taylor Coleridge's poem, "The Rime of the Ancient Mariner" (1798), and the "intense solitude in the clear frozen North—nature in her utter loneliness": "To the right rise masses of ice—blue islands in a blue sea; amid them a turquoise arch over a sapphire current,—but all is ice and the fearful silence of intensest cold. It is not the burning sulphur blue which the sea wears in the warm Mediterranean, and sends up in mad light like the chemical fires of a theatre into the *Grottona Azzura* of Capri. It is another light and another life here; but always real and always beautiful."

"Fine Arts in New York." *Boston Daily Evening Transcript,* April 10, 1861, 4.

[Winthrop, Theodore?]. "The Lounger. Church's New Picture." *Harper's Weekly* (New York), April 20, 1861, 242–243.

". . . the picture which we have all known was painting for us: the new work of the year, which is as surely and sternly required of a famous painter as of a successful novelist. There it is, at last. . . . It is as bold a picture as was ever painted, for there is nothing before you but air, light, and water."

Reviews of Noble's After Icebergs with a Painter

Noble, Louis Legrand. *After Icebergs with a Painter: A Summer Voyage to Labrador and Around Newfoundland.* New York: D. Appleton and Company; London: Sampson Low and Son, 1861.

"'Icebergs! Icebergs!'—The cry brought us upon deck at sunrise. There they were, two of them, a large one and a smaller: the latter pitched upon the dark and misty desert of the sea like an Arab's tent; and the larger like a domed mosque in marble of a greenish white. The vaporous atmosphere veiled its sharp outlines, and gave it a softened, dreamy and mysterious character. Distant and dim, it was yet very grand and impressive. Enthroned on the deep in lonely majesty, the dread of mariners, and the wonder of the traveller, it was one of those imperial creations of nature that awaken powerful emotions, and illumine the imagination. Wonderful structure! Fashioned by those fingers that wrought the glittering fabrics of the upper deep, and launched upon those adamantine ways into Arctic seas, how beautiful, how strong and terrible! A glacier slipped into the ocean, and henceforth a wandering cape, a restless headland, a revolving island, to compromise the security of the world's broad highway." (28–29)

"In the seams and fissures the shadows are the softest blue of the skies, and as plain and palpable as smoke. It melts at every pore, and streams as if a perpetually overflowing fountain were upon the summit, and flashes and scintillates like one vast brilliant. Prongs and reefs of ice jutting from the body of the berg below, and over which we pass, give the water that emerald clearness so lovely to the eye, and open to view something like the fanciful sea-green caves. . . . Its water-line, under which the waves disappear in a lengthy, piazza-like cavern, with explosive sounds, is certainly a remarkable feature." (108)

"While in the act of sketching, C— suddenly exclaimed: when, lo! walls and towers were falling asunder, and tumbling at various angles with apparent silence into the ocean, attended with the most prodigious dashing and commotion of water. Enormous sheaves of foam sprung aloft and burst in air; high, green waves, crested with white-caps, rolled away in circles, mingling with leaping shafts and fragments of ice reappearing from the deep in all directions. Nearly the whole of this brilliant spectacle was the performance of a minute, and to us as noiseless as the motions of a cloud, for a length of time I had not expected. When the uproar reached us, it was thunder doubled and redoubled, rolling upon the car like the quick successive strokes of a drum, or volleys of the largest ordnance. It was awfully grand, and altogether the most startling exhibition I ever witnessed. At this moment, there is a large field of ruins, some of them huge masses like towers prone along the waters, with a lofty steeple left alone standing in the midst, and rocking slowly to and fro." (186–87)

World (New York), April 11, 1861, 3.

New York Journal of Commerce, April 20, 1861, 2.

Morning Courier and New-York Enquirer, April 23, 1861, 2.

Philadelphia Daily Evening Bulletin, April 23, 1861, 1.

Home Journal (New York), April 27, 1861, 4.

Albion (New York), April 27, 1861, 201.

Providence (R.I.) Daily Journal, May 8, 1861, 1.

New-York Daily Tribune, May 12, 1861, 2.

Newark (N.J.) Daily Advertiser, May 17, 1861, 2.

New York Evening Post, May 27, 1861, 1.

Daily Alta California (San Francisco), May 28, 1861, 2.

Ladies' Repository (Cincinnati), June 1861, 379.

New Englander and Yale Review (New Haven) 19 (July 1861): 781–782.

North American Review (Boston) 93 (July 1861): 289.

Athenaeum (London), September 21, 1861, 368–370.

Saturday Review (London), October 12, 1861, 386–387.

Examiner (London), October 26, 1861, 678–679.

Eclectic Review (London), November 1861, 595–602.

Guardian (London), November 6, 1861, 1022.

Critic (London), November 9, 1861, 472–473.

Littell's Living Age (Boston) 71 (December 7, 1861): 472–476.

Reprints of the London *Saturday Review* and *Examiner* reviews.

Eclectic Magazine of Foreign Literature, Science and Art (New York) 55 (January 1862): 94–98.

Christian Examiner (Boston) 72 (May 1862): 368–383.

Reviews of The Icebergs, *New York Debut, 1861*

Copies of more than two dozen published previews, reviews, and poems dedicated to the picture from all three cities were clipped for a scrapbook that Church owned (formerly at Olana; unlocated), of which photocopies have been preserved.

"The Icebergs." *New-York Daily Tribune*, April 24, 1861, 7.

"Art." *Morning Courier and New-York Enquirer*, April 25, 1861, 2.

[Tuckerman, Henry T.]. "Fine Arts. A Trio of Pictures. Church's Icebergs." *New-York Evening Post*, April 25, 1861, 1.

"Literature and Art." *New York Leader*, April 27, 1861, 6.

"Mr. Church's Picture." *New York Morning/Evening Express*, April 27, 1861, 2, 1.

"Icebergs of the North." *New York Journal of Commerce*, April 29, 1861, 2.

"The North." *World* (New York), April 29, 1861, 5.

"Upon ordinary occasions a new picture by Mr. CHURCH would be for a time an object of central attention to the cultivated community of New York. At present the war excitement absorbs every other, and the picture of the 'Icebergs' has been placed on view at GOUPIL'S without attracting especial attention. Last year the announcement of such a work would have packed the gallery from morning till night for weeks; now so intense and eager is the interest concentrated upon the capital, the movements of the forces, and the pageantry wherein the town has draped itself, that we doubt if any considerable number of our citizens are aware of its exhibition. . . . [T]he 'Icebergs' lead us at once to the inner arcana of that mysterious temple which sits forever upon the forehead of the world. We can but stand at the base of that towering cliff of ice, broken into huge crystallizations of form, streaked with mingled tints of azure, emerald and gray, kindling here and there into cold, intense gleams of dazzling luster, and look out along the lazy folds of water towards the white pinnacles, uplifted against the horizon, and confess the picture is above and beyond criticism. . . . We think it will require some time to get even on speaking terms with the 'Icebergs'. They are not taken into the soul with a glance. We shall be surprised if those of acute sensibilities do not look upon it at first with a positive feeling of pain, akin to that which we sometimes feel in the presence of the terrible visions of sleep."

Proteus. "'There is a North'—Church's Last Work." *New-York Commercial Advertiser*, April 29, 1861, 2.

"Sketchings. Domestic Art Gossip." *Crayon* 8 (May 1861): 116.

Mentions that Church's *Icebergs* will be the first work shown in the new second-floor room of Goupil's Gallery on Broadway at Ninth Street.

Cuyler, The Rev. Theodore L. "Among the Icebergs." *Independent* (New York), May 2, 1861, 1.

M.C.A. "From New York. From Our Own Correspondent. New York, May 2." *Springfield (Mass.) Daily Republican*, May 4, 1861, 1.

"... Goupil's Gallery has recently been fitted up with most artistic beauty, and here crowds are flocking to look at Church's great painting of 'The North,' exhibited for the benefit of 'the Patriotic Fund.' Goupil's Gallery, last winter, was most disgracefully cold and dismal; now it is most harmonious and genial. Its floor is covered with a carpet of deep emerald which has the soothing effect of turf under your feet. It is furnished with sofas and divans of a rich purple maroon, and the walls are hung with soft cloth of the same hue. At the end of the gallery, beneath sweeping drapery, within a massive frame of dark, gorgeously carved wood, glitter the scintillant ice-bergs, and gleams, freezing as it flows far out to arctic solitudes, the emerald and azure ocean of the North. Such a picture was never painted before in this or any other country. It is not a picture, it is a sublime fact. You forget the gallery, the ostentatious frame, to sail out unawares into one of God's primeval solitudes. The Alpine peaks, which splinter their sheen around you, shoot from one mighty berg, which unites below the surface of the sea. On the left is overhanging, precipitous ice,—its whiteness belted with sapphire, mottled with reflected lights of intense emerald; with dark blues made from white ice under shadows; with bands of pale blue formed of transparent ice in the cracks of the glaciers. Before you rises an immense hight [*sic*] with all its grand ice-architecture; great boulders have recently fallen from its sides, and lie on the white, solitary shore. All the foreground has risen from the waves; here is a dark rock, caught in the pearly ice, and here a bridge and arch of ice, under which the green waters break in grassy [*sic*] circles. Through an ice-walled avenue, the path of the sea widens with stiffening swell out to the far horizon, where, silent and distant, other ice mountains gleam against the opaque solitude of sky. The brightness of the iceberg so affects the eye that the sea darkens in the distance to violet, while nearer it reflects all the emerald and azure of the mountains above. In a dull light, the iceberg is a dead white, ghastly and spiritless, but in the full sun it kindles with all the splendor of the prismatic hues. Here we see icebergs in their most brilliant hour. Violet shadows drift over the long reaches of pearl. Lights, hues, tints, warm and tender, flit and shimmer over gorge and cliff. Over the frozen heart of this grand ice solitude palpitates warmth and color. Its stupendous crests of crystal are swept by swift, luminous mist, while the infinite sky, somber and solitary, bends over all the resplendent solitude of ice and ocean."

"Icebergs of the North." *New York Journal of Commerce*, May 2, 1861, 2.

Providence (R.I.) Daily Journal, May 2, 1861, 2.

Chicago Daily Tribune, May 4, 1861, 2.

"Fine Arts. Mr. Church among the Icebergs." *Albion* (New York), May 4, 1861, 213.

"Ordinary observers ... may perhaps experience some slight disappointment when they miss all familiar objects and find no trace whatever of human association, not a living creature of any description, no ship, no boat, not even the semblance of a wreck, no connecting link of any sort between themselves and the canvas. One brown boulder of rock, lodged on the ice, alone hints that the great floating glacier was once in contact with earth. There is, so to speak, a complete abnegation of extrinsic interest. ... In conclusion, we ... beg that impulsive visitors, apt to form impressions at the first glance, will sit patiently awhile before this remarkable attempt to grapple with the heretofore unapproached. It cannot be grasped off-hand; yet a sense of its beauty and power will probably grow on those, who study it with deliberation and earnestness."

"Art Items." *New-York Daily Tribune*, May 5, 1861, 3.

"Personal." *Home Journal* (New York), May 11, 1861, 2.

"The Bostonian in New-York." *New-York Daily Tribune*, May 12, 1861, 3.

"... To return to the studio [of Church], we see a glory of a butterfly hung in a frame on the wall, and before we look at the picture the artist shows us another, with an exquisite opalline luster, like burnished crystal, hiding a thought of heaven. We soon understand the value of this beautiful toy of nature, for when the large canvas on the easel is turned toward us, and the iceberg appears in its living portrait, we see prevailing over its varied colors a sheen like the luster on the butterfly's wing. The painter had assisted his memory by this little memorandum of nature, fortuitously met with, but when found, to be made a note of. This wonderful combination of color had been tried, let us imagine, on the insect's wing, and then transferred to the larger labor of the iceberg, and the artist had found and followed the process. I will not prejudge the picture, whose merit seems to me indisputable, but whose composition does not give much scope for descriptive particularization. It is an iceberg, a thing of extraordinary prismatic beauty, with the sea about it, and only a vista of eternal Winter in its rear. As we studied its various aspects, we rejoiced in the well-heated stove of the studio. The picture is one that would affect the thermometer, and lower the temperature of the exhibition room, say twenty degrees. Tacitus says that in all defeats the *eye* is conquered first. So, in all Arctic freezings, the eye feels the first shock, and anticipates in a moment the slow agonies that shall wind slowly, enduringly about the tender tissues, and the unsuspecting blood vessels. This first shock, Mr. Church's picture gives us."

"Sonnet to F.E.C." *New York Evening Express*, May 13, 1861, 2.

Boston Daily Evening Transcript, May 27, 1861, 1, 2.

"Sketchings. Domestic Art Gossip." *Crayon* 8 (June 1861): 133.

"Fine Arts." *New-York Commercial Advertiser,* June 10, 1861, 2.

Daily Alta California (San Francisco), June 14, 1861, 1.

"Art Intelligence." *New-York Commercial Advertiser,* June 18, 1861, 2.

"Fine Arts." *New York Herald,* June 19, 1861, 4.

"American Art." *Knickerbocker* (New York), July 1861, 50.

> "None need be told that Church is great—that he is national. Has he not given us his 'Niagara' and his 'Heart of the Andes,' and is he not treating us this summer with his refrigerating 'Iceberg?' How those dazzling mountains of ice freeze into the very soul, awing us with the mystic revelations of another sphere!"

"Editor's Easy Chair." *Harper's New Monthly Magazine,* July 1861, 266.

Rossetti, William Michael, in *Weldon's Register of Facts and Occurrences Relating to Literature, the Sciences, and the Arts* (London), August 1861, 94.

Reviews of The Icebergs, *Boston, 1862*

The North. Painted by F. E. Church, from Studies of Icebergs made in the Northern Seas in the Summer of 1859, broadside (Boston: Prentiss & Deland, Printers, 1862). No copies of the New York edition (1861) of the broadside are now known.

"Church's New Picture." *Boston Daily Evening Transcript,* February 21, 1862, 2.

Boston Daily Journal, February 22, 1862, 1.

K. C. "Picture Galleries." *Christian Register* (Boston), February 22, 1862, 26.

"Local Matters. Church's 'North.'" *Daily Advertiser* (Boston), February 22, 1862, 1.

"Boston and Vicinity. Art Matters." *Boston Daily Journal,* March 1, 1862, 2.

"Church's 'North.'" *Saturday Evening Gazette* (Boston), March 1, 1862, 2.

"The North—A Picture of Icebergs." *Boston Post,* March 1, 1862, 4.

"The Artists' Exhibition." *Boston Daily Evening Transcript,* March 4, 1862, 2.

> "Here we have floating islands of ice illuminated by the setting sun, in a purple sea, and with every conceivable fracture, form and color—emerald arches under which the sea flows, lofty forms of pure, glowing white, suggesting the great white throne of the Apocalypse."

"Church's New Picture: 'The North.'" *Boston Daily Evening Transcript,* March 11, 1862, 1.

> Longest notice in the *Transcript.*

K. C. "Church's Picture of 'The North.'" *Christian Register* (Boston), March 15, 1862, 42.

> "I have heard persons complain that they never dreamed dreams and saw visions: now, then, is their opportunity. They can go to the Athenæum and look at Church's picture of 'The North.' It will burst on their sense like a vision, it will follow them home and haunt them for weeks, it may open their eyes to finer visions. . . . Consider what an iceberg is; something between the cumulus clouds of June, and the shifting Aurora of a January night. . . . The sides of the berg are like cloven mother-of-pearl; there are crags of sapphire, and cliffs of fretted opal. The tints are mystic and lovely as the tinge inside of a white rose; the shades soft as those between petals of waterlilies. . . . I have told you nothing of the opaline lustres, the chase of rainbows over the surfaces 'white as no fuller on earth can white' them—the mystery of faint, changeful shadows; nor have I mentioned the accumulations of graceful and suggestive form, arch, spire, column, statue, vase, shell. Look for yourself, and you will henceforth gaze at the North Star with more respect, since it points to a continent of waters filled with these icy cathedrals, where ocean is choir, and solitude priest, and beauty the moving presence of the Lord. Truly 'there is an evangel in art as well as books,' and Church is among the prophets."

"Landscape Painting." *Saturday Evening Gazette* (Boston), March 22, 1862, 1.

Parker, H. W. "The Iceberg." *Daily Evening Traveller* (Boston), March 27, 1862, 1.

> A poem submitted by a reader who had seen the painting. Another poem, dated March 1862, "The North—a Painting by Church," from an unspecified—and, presumably, Boston—journal, was in Church's scrapbook.

"Church's Picture of the North." *Boston Daily Evening Transcript,* March 28, 1862, 2.

"Exhibition of Paintings." *Boston Daily Evening Transcript,* April 2, 1862, 2.

"After Icebergs with a Painter." *Christian Examiner* (Boston), 72 (May 1862): 368–383.

> ". . . 'The North,' that vision of wonder and beauty, that dreamy lotos of Arctic seas, with a loveliness as strange, penetrating and ethereal as the fragrance of Arctic flowers. It is a frozen Aurora Borealis, with temples of white dissolving flame, with pillars of pearl, and vanishing wings of angels at its doors, or glowing in the sunset light above. By mere touches of color and form the picture hints how all the separate, scattered beauty of the world is gathered and heaped confusedly in those lone Northern seas, as if they were Beauty's working-room and studio, where she plans Parthenons and 'Peter's domes,' and models with sure, quick fingers her oriels and Byzantine columns, her vase-like flowers, and flower-like shells,—yea, stains them with dyes such as they of Tyre knew not. . . . And back of book and picture our thoughts are led, to find how like children we are amused and educated in this world. God throws the words down in confusion, and we assort them into epics, and are flattered. We are elated, but the angels smile." (376–377)

"Pen, Pallet, and Piano." *Continental Monthly* (New York), January 1863, 117, 121.

"Church's Cotopaxi." *New York Times*, March 17, 1863, 4.

"Cotopaxi." *World* (New York), March 18, 1863, 4.

"Art Talk." *New York Evening Express*, March 31, 1863, 2.

"Minor Topics of the Month." *London Art-Journal*, May 1, 1863, 102.

Reviews of The Icebergs, *London, 1863*

"From Our Private Correspondent. London, Thursday Morning." *Manchester Guardian*, June 19, 1863, 2.

"I have never seen anything like the singularly truthful and delicate painting of the prismatic effects of light on these monstrous masses of opaque ice; indeed, no such painting has been seen. It is altogether a most weird and beautiful picture; one to affect the imagination powerfully by virtue of its grand and simple truth. Let all your readers who love art, and visit London, take care to see this picture. I have no fear of their charging me with exaggeration."

"Fine Arts. Mr. Church's Icebergs." *Observer* (London), June 21, 1863, 6.

"It may be pretty safely anticipated that his [Church's] icebergs will become the summer resort of all London."

"Fine Arts. German; Gallery, Bond Street." *Morning Herald* (London), June 22, 1863, 7.

"Fine Arts. German Gallery, Bond Street." *Standard* (London), June 22, 1863, 6.

"Mr. Church's Picture of Icebergs." *Morning Advertiser* (London), June 22, 1863, 6.

"The Iceberg—Painted by Church." *Morning Star* (London), June 22, 1863, 3.

"The Iceberg—Painted by Church." *Evening Star* (London), June 22, 1863, 2.

"Fine Arts. An Iceberg Picture." *Daily News* (London), June 25, 1863, 3.

". . . The spectator may imagine himself standing upon the foreground ice like one saved from a wreck, for at his feet there is the topmast and top with part of a torn sail, all that is left of some gallant ship crushed in the terrific charge of two of these floating mountains."

"Metropolitan On Dits." *Court Journal* (London), June 27, 1863, 633.

"Mr. Church's 'Icebergs.'" *Athenaeum* (London), June 27, 1863, 847.

"Such ice-borne boulders are said to be the originals of our enormous stones that, grouped by some forgotten people to serve priestly rites, are named Druidic temples or tombs. The stone, deeply tinged with iron, has stained with red and russet streaks the pure snow and ice of its bed."

"Notes on Art. American Artists." *Sunday Times* (London), June 28, 1863, 2.

"Minor Topics of the Month." *London Art-Journal*, July 1, 1863, 147.

"Mr. Church's Ice Picture," July 1, 1863.

Clipping from an unidentified London publication, in Church scrapbook, dated by annotation, July 1.

[Taylor, Tom]. "Mr. Church's Picture of Icebergs." *London Times*, July 3, 1863, 12.

"The picture altogether is a noble example of that application of the landscape-painter's art to the rendering of grand, beautiful and unfamiliar aspects of nature, only accessible at great cost of fatigue and exposure, and even at the peril of life and limb, which seems to be one of the walks in which this branch of the art is destined to achieve new triumphs in our time. All who can honour and appreciate the art in this new and arduous development of it should see Mr. Church's great picture."

"Fine Arts. Iceberg Picture." *Court Journal* (London), July 4, 1863, 664.

"Fine Arts. Church's Picture of Icebergs." *Illustrated London News*, July 4, 1863, 7.

"A band of purest azure will next arrest the eye, and this, we are told, must have been a great fissure or crevasse, in which the thawed water has again frozen, the purest blue being the well-known result of light passing into, as well as through, a limpid medium of great depth. Next, another crevasse will be noticed, not filled up, however, but emitting the loveliest emerald light. This, our Arctic friends will know, arises from the light being transmitted partly through and again reflected from the sea beneath, or the semi-transparent compacted snows and ice of the berg."

"Mr. Church's Picture." *Court Circular* (London), July 4, 1863, 523.

Rawlinson, Robert. "Icebergs and Meteorology." *London Times*, July 7, 1863, 7.

Wallich, G. C. "Icebergs and Meteorology." *London Times*, July 8, 1863, 6.

"Fine Arts. A Painter among the Icebergs." *London Review*, July 11, 1863, 49.

"Church's 'Icebergs' in England." *World* (New York), July 14, 1863, 8.

"The State of Europe. From France. From Our Own Correspondent. Paris, June 26, 1863." *New-York Daily Tribune*, July 15, 1863, 3.

"Art. Mr. Church's Picture of Icebergs." *Reader* (London), July 18, 1863, 67–68.

"Fine Arts." *Albion* (New York), July 18, 1863, 345.

"Table Talk." *Guardian* (London), July 29, 1863, 720.

"Epitome of the Week. Art, Science, and Literature." *Leslie's Illustrated Newspaper* (New York), August 1, 1863, 295.

"Fine Arts. Mr. Church's Icebergs.—Mr. Hamerton's Pictures." *Spectator*, August 1, 1863, 2320.

"Minor Topics of the Month." *London Art-Journal*, August 1, 1863, 167.

Hall, Major H. Byng. "Art in America." *St. James's Magazine* (London), September 1863, 240.

Reprinted in *Albion* (New York), September 19, 1863, 453.

"... For hours I have watched his pencil working on the canvas [*Icebergs*], and all who look on his picture must alike admit the interest of the subject and the talent of the artist.... The 'Icebergs' seen in London radiate upon the spectator an atmosphere of cold. There is not a pulse of life upon the canvas;—nothing but glittering precipices of ice, and rugged summits hoary with snow, and desolate reaches of water."

W[illiam] P. B[ayley]. "Mr. Church's Picture of 'The Icebergs.'" *London Art-Journal*, September 1, 1863, 187–188.

"It is the heart of the *Icebergs* you have been brought now. The wondrous, floating, sailing Alps of Ice soar around you everywhere, drearily terrible, no doubt, in their commoner aspect; but the adventurous painter has been permitted to hang over them leisurely, in those moments when the glowing colours of summer evening air soften them, through their intense reflective power, with delicate beauties of even an oriental and fairy-like splendour..."

Rossetti, William Michael. "Art-Exhibitions in London." *Fine Arts Quarterly Review* (London), October 1863, 343.

Later Mentions of The Icebergs, *1863–1879*

"Frederic Edwin Church. Phrenological Character and Biography." *American Phrenological Journal and Life Illustrated* (New York), 38 (October 1863): 91.

"A Retrospect of Art in 1863." *Reader* (London), January 2, 1864, 23.

"A National Gallery of Paintings." *Boston Daily Evening Transcript*, January 17, 1865, 1.

"'Chimborazo' has been sold to a party in London, and is now on its way to that city. It is insured in New York, for something like $15,000, and is therefore doubtless disposed of at that amount. Mr. Church has also sold his master work, the 'Icebergs,' to a member of Parliament at about the same price.... Mr. Church fell into the hands of a publisher of great experience, and sufficient means to have his works re-produced, in the very highest style, either of line engraving or in chromotography.... he has achieved an enviable fame and a great financial success by the sale and copy-right of his work.... and, further, that but thirty copies of the 'Icebergs' chromos remain for subscribers." In fact, *Chimborazo* (1864, The Huntington Library, Art Collections, and Botanical Gardens, San Marino, Calif.) was purchased by an American collector, Samuel Hallett, for a sum closer to $5,000. It is not known for how much Church sold *The Icebergs*.

"Icebergs. Painted by F. Church. Chromolithographed by Charles Risdon. Published by Day and Son, London." *London Art-Journal*, March 1, 1865, 96.

"... The subject is treated with so much reality that we absolutely shiver before it. The scene is apart from humanity, existing in its lonely grandeur far away from the foot-paths of man. No doubt the artist has called imagination to his aid; but the picture carries with it a conviction of truth; there seems no exaggeration in those singular or grotesque forms reflecting all the hues that glorify a rainbow. Messrs. Day have issued no production that so conclusively exhibits the power of their Art—none that so effectively shows what can be done by the appliances at their command. We cannot say to how many 'printings' it has been subjected; but they must have been very numerous; for, perhaps, there has never been a chromolithograph containing so many 'tints.'"

"Fine Arts. Mr. Church's Pictures of Chimborazo and Cotopaxi." *London Daily News*, June 19, 1865, 7.

"Fine Arts. American Landscapes." *London Review*, June 24, 1865, 662.

[Taylor, Tom]. "Mr. F. E. Church's New Pictures." *London Times*, June 28, 1865, 6.

"Art. Church's New Pictures of Chimborazo and Cotopaxi." *Reader* (London), July 1, 1865, 18–19.

"Fine Arts." *Court Journal* (London), July 15, 1865, 712.

Bayley, W. P. "Mr. Church's Pictures. Cotopaxi, Chimborazo, and the Aurora Borealis, Considered also with Reference to English Art." *London Art-Journal*, September 1, 1865, 265.

H.B.H. "A Visit to the Studios of Some American Artists." *London Art-Journal*, December 1, 1865, 362.

Tuckerman, Henry T. "Frederic Edwin Church." *Galaxy: An Illustrated Magazine of Entertaining Reading* (New York), July 1866, 422.

Hayes, Isaac I. *The Open Polar Sea: A Narrative of a Voyage of Discovery towards the North Pole in the Schooner "United States"* (New York: Hurd and Houghton, 1867), 25–26.

"... nothing indeed but the pencil of the artist could depict the wonderful richness of this sparkling fragment of Nature. Church, in his great picture of 'The Icebergs,' has grandly exhibited a scene not unlike that which I would in vain describe."

Tuckerman, Henry T. *Book of the Artists: American Artist Life. Comprising Biographical and Critical Sketches of American Artists: Preceded by an Historical Account of the Rise & Progress of Art in America* (New York: G. P. Putnam and Son; London: Sampson Low and Son, 1867; reprint, New York: James F. Carr, 1967), 380–384.

"When the idea of making icebergs the subject of a picture suggested itself to Mr. Church, it was but the un-conscious response to the curiosity and wonder which arctic discovery had excited in the public mind. . . . Accordingly he desired, if possible, to make his canvas reflect the glint and gloom, the grandeur and beauty, the coldness and desolation of the north. . . .

It was a hazardous experiment. . . . Ice—water—sky—these elements alone, to most painters, would afford little scope for general effect, however much they may be rendered of special significance.

Church looked steadily at the facts of nature, and believed that form, color, and arrangement could be made to give to these objects, in combination, somewhat of the impressive and unique charm they wear in reality to the keen observer and the imaginative vision . . . he determined to study icebergs where they may be seen to the best advantage, viz., off the coast of Labrador.

Returning with a mass of sketches, outlines, studies in oil, and above all, his mind clearly and fully stored with picturesque material, Church went to work with that intrepid zeal that belongs to his nature, and then produced the picture which, while it adds a new and permanent trophy to his fame, conserves and diffuses an authentic and interesting revelation of a phenomenon of nature—comparatively unfamiliar, yet infinitely suggestive. Church's picture typifies the north. He has combined, as far as possible in one view, the most characteristic forms and colors. The centre berg—the slope of the melting mass, the glint of the upright drift, the transparent blue, the opal gleam, the sapphire refraction, the cliff-like shape, the pearly edge, the glittering stalactite, the opaque alabaster line, the ice-paved sea, the cold atmosphere and pale sky-flush,—all we have read and imagined of such a scene, is here brought together with scientific conscientiousness and artistic skill and taste.

The result is novel. As we gaze, the truth and meaning of the picture grow upon eye and mind, as nature does, until admiration fairly takes us captive. All spectators of true observation will appreciate the artistic power and the truth of nature; but few will rightly estimate the difficulties overcome, the patient study involved in this work."

"Frederic Edwin Church." *Harper's Weekly* (New York), June 8, 1867, 364.

[Bayley, W. P.]. "Fine Arts. Mr. Church's Damascus." *London Morning Post*, June 24, 1869, 6.

"American Painters.—Frederick [*sic*] Edwin Church, N.A." *American Art-Journal* (New York), March 1878, 67.

French, H. W. *Art and Artists in Connecticut*. (Boston: Lee & Shepard; New York, Charles T. Dillingham, 1879; reprint, New York: Da Capo Press, 1970), 130, 133–134.

"American Painters.—Frederick [*sic*] Edwin Church, N.A." *London Art-Journal*, November 1879, 240.

8

8 Exquisite opalescent bluegreen

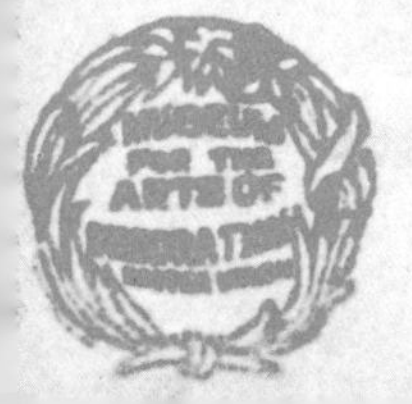